Endorsements

Women will DEVOUR this book. Some might even sleep with it under their pillow. It brings beautiful comfort and rich insight from a friend who understands the heartbreak of infertility and miscarriage. Amanda hands us women a true GIFT with the words of this book."

—Lysa TerKeurst, *New York Times* best-selling author of *Unglued* and president of Proverbs 31 Ministries

A calming and peaceful portal into the lives of families suffering from infertility with an approach of stoic surrender and acceptance of God's will. Soothing to the soul!

—Elizabeth Maxwell, MD

BARREN

among the

Fruitful

BARREN

among the

Fruitful

NAVIGATING INFERTILITY
with HOPE, WISDOM, and PATIENCE

AMANDA HOPE HALEY

THOMAS NELSON
Since 1798

NASHVILLE   DALLAS   MEXICO CITY   RIO DE JANEIRO

Published in Nashville, Tennessee, by Thomas Nelson. Thomas Nelson is a registered trademark of HarperCollins Christian Publishing, Inc.

Page design and layout: Crosslin Creative

Thomas Nelson titles may be purchased in bulk for educational, business, fund-raising, or sales promotional use. For information, please e-mail SpecialMarkets@ThomasNelson.com.

Scripture quotations are taken from The Voice™ translation. © 2012 Ecclesia Bible Society. Used by permission. All rights reserved.

ISBN: 978-1-4016-7975-0

Printed in the United States of America

14 15 16 17 18 [RRD] 6 5 4 3 2 1

For our precious godsons, Elijah and Jack.
You unknowingly snuggled David and
me during the coldest years of our lives.

Acknowledgments

I never planned to write this book, so I had no idea what I was doing when the publishing process began. There is no way I could have finished this manuscript without the input and guidance of my editor and friend, Maleah Bell; but I wouldn't have started it without the encouragement and faith of my publisher, mentor, and friend, Frank Couch. Everyone at Thomas Nelson is a consummate professional, but you two are the best of them. I am blessed to be learning from you.

I was inspired by my dear friends and relatives, who sacrificially told me their personal stories for this book. You each reopened wounds to share your pain and perspective with women suffering as you have; then you prayed for me and all the readers who will encounter your stories. I love you all.

Way back in 2002 my best friend and adopted sister, Melinda Phillips, dreamed I was an archaeologist in Israel and a mother of four children. You saw David arriving at my dig site fresh off a plane—gathering our daughter in his arms, kissing me, and corralling our three unruly boys. You dreamt of the life I wanted, but I know you agree that God has planned a journey better than we imagined. Thank you for choosing to stick with me through my decade of insanity.

No one has given me more prayer support through the writing process and through my life as a whole than my parents-in-law, Robert and Julie Haley. You prayed for me before you met me, you knew I'd married David even before he did, and you've loved me not as your daughter-in-law but as your daughter. Thank you for being the best second set of parents a girl could have.

My parents, Ross and Dana Womack, traveled this road of infertility more than two decades before David and I did. If you hadn't sought medical help, I would not be here. I thank you for the literal life you gave to me, the instruction that made me into the adult I am today, and the selfless love I always feel from you no matter how far apart we are.

David Haley is my darling husband and one true love. You tell me I can do anything, and you help me achieve any goal I set. I am genuinely thankful that I wake up next to you each morning and that this crazy journey has pushed us together instead of pulling us apart. I know the next eleven years of marriage will be better than the first as we continue to grow together with God's blessing over us.

Contents

Foreword

My heart aches for my daughter and son-in-law as they deal with the struggles brought on by infertility. Amanda's father and I tried for several years to conceive a child after we first married. We did not have the medical options then that are available today. Of course, we were advised to do the typical procedures of that time: check my body temperature regularly for that all-important timing and keep a daily chart. My husband needed to go through the embarrassing ordeal of sperm testing, and he was told to switch from briefs to boxer shorts. We tried these "scientific" approaches. Nothing worked.

One day I went to see my gynecologist for a regular checkup. Looking at my charts, he blurted out, "You haven't ovulated! Let's put you on fertility pills." My thoughts ran amok. We had found the reason that I had not conceived after trying for four years. Wonderful! And now, just maybe there would be a solution. But at what price? Could my baby have birth defects? I well remembered the thalidomide scandal of the 1960s. I was promised that fertility drugs were safe. Would I have multiple births? My doctor assured me that within the time period his team had been using the drug Clomid, they had delivered eight sets of twins and no multiple births larger than twins. So, twins . . . I could handle that. In fact I would welcome that!

I went home from the doctor's office and discussed this with my husband. We decided we must give the pills a try. After taking the pills for two months, I was pregnant. It seemed like a miracle. After seven months of extreme nausea, two months of not-so-bad nausea, and fourteen hours of labor, Amanda Hope Womack was born. She was six pounds, seven ounces, and nineteen inches long. All of her digits were where they were supposed to be, and there was only one of her. The good Lord had truly blessed us with this beautiful little redhead.

Now that our only child is an adult and of childbearing age, I must admit I often wonder if the very pills that enabled me to become pregnant with Amanda caused her to have her own issues with infertility. It is always easy to see new medical breakthroughs as God's will. However, that gnawing thought that maybe we did not trust God enough to let Him take care of our infertility problem in His own way is omnipresent. On the other hand, were the fertility pills God's solution for my and millions of other women's infertility? With more questions than answers, I simply must remember that God is always in charge of everything. His plan is perfect.

After Amanda and David married, we turned Amanda's childhood bedroom into a study for my husband. At this point, I decided to do a little more "updating" of the house. Using pretty pastels, I turned one guest bedroom into a room for my future granddaughters. Amanda had collected porcelain dolls as a child. Since she had no room in her house for them, and with her approval, I displayed them in an antique case. I bought a daybed with a trundle and made pretty pillows, a dust ruffle, and drapes. I even found a white ruffled bassinet at an antique store and secretly tucked it away for future use. Then, in the room directly across the hall, I expanded an existing hunt theme to include things for a little boy. Amanda's own Jenny Lind crib in the attic would be perfect in this room when the time came for grandbabies to sleep here. So whenever Amanda and David decided to start a family, I was ready.

My first cousin is an only child. (Her mother, my mother's sister, had a stillborn baby, followed by several miscarriages. Finally little Robin, a seven-month preemie, was born.) Robin now has three healthy adult sons and her first grandson. After David and Amanda married, whenever anyone asked David how many children they planned to have, he would say, "As many as the Lord blesses us with." Their dream, my dream also, was that children would come as they had for Robin. This dream has not been realized as many of us assumed it would be.

When normal human functions become impossibilities, one must look to other means of fulfillment rather than raising a family in the traditional way. My husband, an elder in our church, performed an infant dedication ceremony one Sunday recently for four families with babies. Our daughter and son-in-law are godparents for one of these infants. They are very proud of and grateful for this honor. The father of this little boy told me after the ceremony that I should have stood up when my husband called for the families of the children to stand. His sweet comment brought such pleasure to my heart. My husband and I are truly proud and blessed to be considered great-godparents to the children of this precious family.

My husband had pseudo-godparents of his own in his aunt and uncle, who have spent their lives loving and caring for family and friends. They eventually became like a third set of grandparents to Amanda. They have given freely of their time and resources to numerous charities: both church- and community-related. They, along with other aunts and uncles on my side of the family who never had children, filled their lives as caregivers. Nothing is more satisfying than helping those in need. I see this as a potential path for David and Amanda. I swell with pride knowing my daughter is using her experiences to write a book that will help others who struggle as she and I both have.

—Dana Womack
Mother of the author

Introduction

Hope Is My Middle Name

If I only had one word to describe myself, it would be *hope*. The Holy Spirit must have whispered that word to my parents before I was born, because that's what they named me: Amanda Hope Womack. I've teased them that it was a blessing and a curse while I grew up, but as I've learned more about what *hope* actually means, I confidently say it is a blessing.

Hope doesn't just mean "wish," as most of us use it these days. To *hope* is to confidently expect that something will happen. I've spent most of my life wishing for very specific things: a proposal from my David, admission to Harvard, safe travel to wherever we're flying, a baby. I thought I was "hoping" for them, but after spending seven years begging God for a child, I learned that God gives us only one hope: reconciliation with Him through the work of Jesus. Jesus is my one hope.

Only recently have I begun to understand fully the blessing that "*Hope* is my middle name."

My young adulthood went smoothly. I met the perfect-for-me man when I was a senior in high school. My David and I married just after we both had graduated from college. (I call him "my David" because it seems as if half of the men in my life are named David. Accidently say, "Hi, sexy" to David—your church administrator—when he calls you one day about Communion bread, and you'll start to differentiate too!)

We kicked off our new life in a no-air-conditioning, crazy-expensive, five-hundred-square-foot, fourth-floor walkup just outside of Boston. I finished my master's degree at Harvard, and we ran back to Tennessee, where we could afford to buy a cute house and start a family. All was moving according to our plans—until that family didn't arrive as we had scheduled.

Over the next seven years, David and I endured two complete rounds of testing, surgery, and treatment at two separate fertility centers. In spite of some really great doctors (and a few not-so-great ones), we had ninety-six cycles of failure. We suffered multiple miscarriages. No one—not even my own mother—knew for certain what was happening with us. All of our family and friends were in Middle Tennessee with us; but it was too painful, too embarrassing, to talk about with anyone but each other.

God used those years to change me inside and out. Trying to make my body whole, I learned the virtues of clean eating and clean products; and saving money for fertility treatments, David and I became debt-free. But these visible improvements were nothing compared to the peace I have now that I hope only in God. Over time my nightly prayer changed from "God, get out of my way" to "God, don't let me get in Your way."

A piece of that journey was unexpectedly traveled with my church family. I worship in a tradition that does not put women in leadership roles; but when my church began organizing life groups for the first time several years ago, the deacons stepped outside tradition and asked me to be a part of the life group leadership team because of my educational background. This resulted in David and me leading a life group for five years in our home, and later in a chapel classroom.

One Sunday morning, after studying a chapter in Ephesians, a friend's unsuspecting husband, whom I was helping with a project, asked about my progress. I reacted by literally collapsing in the floor and crying ugly tears. His innocent question felt like the last straw in my life. David wasn't there. I had just had another miscarriage, work was stressful, my father was recovering from a heart attack, and I had watched David's beloved grandfather die just weeks earlier. It was the first time I was unable to explain away an emotional outburst in public (and there had been many in the years I took hormones). I eventually responded to the shocked faces of my closest friends with three words, "I'm in therapy," as if that explained everything. For me, it did. Admitting that I was seeking professional psychological help was my rock bottom. At that very moment God met me there on the floor; two of the wives physically picked me up off the floor by my shoulders and told me that they, too, were in therapy. Others had been to psychologists in the past. Sharing my pain with them made those burdens so much lighter; the relief was immediate.

As David and I slowly started sharing the story of our previous seven years, I became a lightning rod for women struggling with infertility. Women would confide their stories to me even if they weren't privy to our situation. In July 2012, I had two friends from that very life group confess to me the same tragedy within eight hours of each other: both had miscarriages the previous day, and both were eight weeks pregnant at the time. Neither knew about the other.

I called David from the quiet of my home office, where I was editing part of The Voice Bible translation. I was disturbed. Shaking. Crying. Confused. Overreacting! But David was patient with me and asked me the strangest question: "If you were to write a book about all this, what would you say?"

I spent the next thirty to forty-five minutes writing. My bright-red pen never left the legal pad; my mind never stopped working. I knew I wanted to write a survey of the topic and not a quick-fix or spiritual-companion book; I knew many of the women with whom I wanted to collaborate on this project; and I knew each chapter would be titled with an off-the-cuff, sometimes hurtful, and often ridiculous comment I heard during my fertility journey. (This includes chapter 3's title. A gynecologist once looked me squarely in the face and very seriously asked me, "Are you sure you're doing it right?" implying David and I hadn't figured out what to do in the bedroom in the first four years of our marriage!)

I left my office exhausted and crashed on the couch for a four-hour nap. I was awakened from a very deep sleep by a publisher at Thomas Nelson who also goes to my church and who knew a lot about my medical history. He was calling to ask me about a ghostwriting project. During our "small talk" (which is always deep), I told him what had happened to our friends and how upset I was that morning; and he said to me, "Would you be interested in writing a book about infertility?" Only then did I tell him about my crazy forty-five minutes and the outline sitting on my desk at that moment. His exact words are burned in my memory: "Polish it up, and send it to me by Friday." I think I sent it to him by the next hour.

That conversation led to me becoming part of the InScribed Collection. I have been so blessed through this writing process to learn from other authors with so much more experience than I have. In a workshop where we were sharing our book visions with one another in February 2013, one of them said, "I wish God had given me this book." It hadn't fully dawned on me until that moment that He has indeed given me these ideas and words. I'm not sure why. But please note that any mistakes in this book are completely mine. I am not a medical doctor, a licensed therapist, or even an ordained minister. I'm just a woman who once rode and has disembarked the infertility train. And now I want to share what I learned through years of pain with others—hoping they can skip some of that pain, realize there is a community of women near them suffering as they are, better understand what is happening around them, maybe laugh a little bit at the absurdity of it all, and go straight to hoping in God for their futures.

I suppose the fairy-tale happy ending to this book would be me sharing with the world that I am finally having a baby, but that won't be happening. Of course, it doesn't hurt that I became a "fairy" godmother along the way. (I'm still waiting to receive my wings and wand—you know who you are!) I know, without a doubt, that Amanda having a baby isn't a happy ending. Amanda finding wholeness by hoping only in God is a happy ending! He used all the pain of infertility to draw me closer to Him and to teach me that lesson. God's plans for our lives are amazing when we let go of our wants and embrace Him. His plans are better than mine. They are better than yours too. That's what I *hope* I have articulated in this book.

CHAPTER ONE

"Just Give It Time"

Discovering There's a Problem

It happens just as soon as you say, "I do." People go from asking, "When are you getting married?" to asking, "When are you having children?" I was a twenty-two-year-old bride standing in the receiving line at my own wedding when I was first smacked with this question. Ignoring the complete impertinence of the person who so boldly invaded my business, I blushed and said something like, "Not until we finish grad school."

Such temporal benchmarks can stall your nosy acquaintances for a while, but eventually they—and you—start to wonder why no baby has come. It was around year four that "When will you?" turned into "Why haven't you?" and my answers became markedly less polite.

It is tempting to say that the tendency for all of us to get into each other's business is a result of social-media culture. We put almost everything about ourselves online, so the world logically assumes it has a right to know the rest. But I contend the digital exhibition of our personal lives only exacerbates humanity's millennia-old concern with procreation (and yes, narcissism, but that's a topic for another book).

Consider God's first words to the first man and woman: "Be fruitful and multiply. Populate the earth" (Gen. 1:28). At the beginning of time, children were necessary to continue the human race, so everyone had a vested interest in every woman's fertility. Once the population started growing, sons were needed to perpetuate family fortunes (Num. 27:8–11) or national monarchies (1 Kings 1:17). When survival—physical, fiscal, or political—is at stake, there is no such thing as privacy. Ladies, your mother-in-law wants to know that the family she gave birth to will last forever (Ruth 4:13–17). That longing is in her DNA, and it's probably coded into yours as well.

In year four I may have understood why others were so nosy, but that didn't make their questions any easier because I didn't know the answers myself. We'd been "not preventing" children for two years, and nothing had happened. At my next annual gynecology appointment, I told my doctor we'd been trying for two years, not knowing I was pushing the panic button. Within a week I was seeing specialists. I was officially scared.

Kristine's Story

Life was good. I had married my college sweetheart, Jason; he had finished law school; and we were back in Chicago, the city we loved. We both had great jobs, wonderful friends, a nourishing church, and supportive families. We had just bought a house with lots of room to grow . . . so it was time to make some babies! Life up to that point had been easy and fun.

It took a few months, and another month, and it was starting to be not so easy and fun. Why wasn't I pregnant yet?

I had polycystic ovary syndrome (PCOS). I was partially relieved to learn I actually had something, but I was mostly discouraged. What did this mean? My normal OB/GYN wasn't really qualified to help, although she suggested I try one round of Clomid. If we couldn't get pregnant on Clomid, then she'd refer me to a specialist.

A light period made me think the Clomid hadn't worked, so Jason and I faced the truth that we were off to the fertility clinic. We treated ourselves to Walker Bros., a Chicago breakfast spot. There we decided that this process is not easy and fun; but we were going to face all this together, strengthened by our faith in God, who had a plan for us.

We met with the infertility specialist, who did some tests and said that once I got my period, we could start the Clomid therapy over again. When my "period" did come, something was different. We found out I was six weeks pregnant.

For one day Jason and I were beyond excited. We kept it to ourselves until the doctors got the results from my blood work, and the next day my hormone levels didn't indicate a healthy pregnancy. I was miscarrying, and no amount of synthetic progesterone could sustain the baby. I got the call at work, and it all felt so unceremonious, impersonal, and just awful. The following weeks were pretty rough.

After a few months we returned to the infertility specialist. He wanted to continue the Clomid regimen and add intrauterine insemination (IUI). We tried Clomid for three months but were only able to have an IUI two months because a January snow day kept us from driving safely to the doctor.

The continued use of Clomid was really harsh on me. I was a mess. Clomid has a long half-life, so remnants of the previous month's dosage were still in my system when I started the next month's prescription. Jason and I were having a really rough time just getting along because of my emotions. I was mean, tearful all the time, angry, and annoyed.

The second month we did the IUI (which was the third month in a row I had taken Clomid), we got a negative pregnancy test. On that same day Jason was laid off from his job. We had to stop the infertility treatments because of money, and I was slightly relieved.

Jason and I regrouped that summer. He didn't have a job, I was finally getting the Clomid out of my body, and we needed that break from all the purpose-driven "trying." We were exhausted.

And I was fully bitter. I couldn't open Facebook without being crushed by another pregnancy announcement from a dear friend or hometown acquaintance. These kind people were just living their lives; they weren't expanding their families just to hurt me! But it felt like it. And it felt as though everyone's life was moving along while ours was staying still.

In the back of my mind, I knew God would take care of us, our miscarried baby was in heaven, and that I shouldn't complain about the life I was blessed to have. But I continued to struggle. I was being shaped by God in so many ways, but that wasn't always clear to me, and my faith wasn't always strong.

In the back of my mind, I knew God would take care of us.

We were at a dead end, so I started reading. Thanks to the Chicago Public Library, I picked up a couple of books about PCOS and the best diet for treating symptoms. I changed my food habits and exercised more. And I felt amazing. I lost about fifteen pounds and had tons of energy. I also started getting my periods regularly, which had not happened since I'd stopped birth control.

After about ten months with my renewed health, a close friend who also had PCOS told me about her new doctor at a university hospital. He had taught her about artificial hormones and other environmental factors that may influence infertility. We could afford a co-pay or two, right?

I scheduled an appointment at the University Medical Center, not a dedicated fertility clinic. The doctor was a skilled clinician in a normal office. As any good doctor would, he listened intently to my situation, and he was thrilled that I was healthier and had more regular cycles because of my eating and exercise regimen. He explained some options but suggested I try another drug therapy before investing in a bunch of tests. The breast cancer medicine Femara, when used off-label in fertility patients, blocks estrogen production and doesn't have many of Clomid's emotional and physical side effects.

I started to feel pregnancy symptoms, but this was nothing new to me or Jason. The past three years had been full of phantom symptoms. I wanted a child so badly that I would read any bump or hiccup as a sign I was expecting. Imagine our surprise when, a month later, the pregnancy test was positive. It was surreal.

Jason and I were cautious throughout the first trimester. We didn't tell people and tried not to get our hopes up again. But on February 24, 2012, over three and a half years after we started trying, Madeline Kristine arrived and all the waiting was over. It was the end of a long road I hope never to travel again, and one I surely will never forget.

"Let's do a few tests . . ."

It all starts easily enough: a blood test here, an ultrasound there. But what the tests can reveal run the spectrum of minor and fixable to dangerous and permanent. What follows is a survey of the most common causes of infertility in women. This list is by no means exhaustive, but it demonstrates how all things in our bodies and world work together to create a sustainable pregnancy.

Age

The first question I was asked at every visit to the fertility clinic was, "How old are you?" As long as I said I was in my twenties, I received a smile and a pat on the knee from the nurse. The implication was that there was nothing to worry about; the fertility clinic could help. Once I hit thirty, no nurse ever smiled again. Without words (and sometimes with them), they accused me of waiting too long to get pregnant and wouldn't make any promises about the clinic's ability to help such an "old" woman. They didn't need me dragging down their live-birth statistics.

While I would love to dismiss the sometimes-callous concern for a woman's age as discrimination, this ageism has been justified by the medical community:

- As a woman's age increases, the time it takes her to get pregnant also increases.

- Women under the age of thirty have a 71 percent chance of conceiving; women over the age of thirty-six have a 41 percent chance.

- For every five years of age, a woman's body is 10 percent more likely to spontaneously abort a pregnancy due to chromosomal abnormalities.[1]

The truth is clear: the younger a woman is, the easier it is to have children. However, women are typically not in control of when they begin a family. What if a woman is thirty before she finishes her education, thirty-five before she reaches career benchmarks, or forty before she gets married? We will look more closely at the social and professional reasons more women are waiting to start a family in chapter 6.

Endometriosis

Affecting 8 to 10 percent of all menstruating women, endometriosis is the most common physical abnormality associated with infertility. In this pathology, uterine tissue is present outside the uterus. Commonly found around the ovaries and fallopian tubes, it has also been known to occur outside the abdomen, even at the base of the brain. It is a stubborn condition that is difficult to diagnose (requiring endoscopic surgery at a hospital) and nearly impossible to treat. One woman can have just a few cells of endometrial tissue and be unable to conceive; another's ovaries could be covered in the tissue but she may never know she has the disease and deliver as many children as she desires.

Of the women diagnosed with endometriosis, approximately 30 percent will be unable to conceive. This may happen for two reasons:

1. Endometrial tissue physically blocks the progress of fetal development, either preventing the egg from moving as it should or so thickening the uterine wall that a fertilized egg cannot implant.

2. Endometrial tissue produces hormones that imbalance the body and prohibit a sustainable pregnancy.

This condition is maddening not just for the woman, but for the doctor as well. Common treatments are hormone therapy and tissue removal, which may or may not allow for conception. Neither targets the source of endometriosis (which is unknown), so most women must wait until menopause to get complete relief from the often-intense abdominal pain and cramping associated with it.[2]

Hormone Imbalance

When David and I jumped on the fertility train for the second time, our practitioner spent twelve months charting us. He took blood regularly and asked that we make significant lifestyle changes to try to balance our hormones naturally. At the top of the to-do list was eliminating artificial hormones from our lives. This meant changing all of our cosmetics and toiletries, eating biodynamically grown foods, repainting our house, installing a whole-house water filter, and replacing all of our floors with wood or natural stone. This was an expensive endeavor that still isn't completely finished six years later, but every change we made was valuable.

Artificial hormones are everywhere, and they are just as dangerous for men as they are for women. You commonly find them in plastics, household dust, air fresheners, preservatives, cosmetics, and medications. It is impossible to avoid all artificial hormones all the time, but chapter 5 will explore how we can limit our contact with them without abandoning all modern conveniences.

Malformation

As my yoga instructor likes to say, "We are all made exactly alike, but with infinite differences." It's an encouraging reminder that not every woman can elegantly twist herself into every shape of pretzel Miss Evelyn prompts, and that I shouldn't push my muscles and spine to the point of injury for fear of not "looking like my neighbor." I may be able to touch the top of my head to the floor in a forward bend, but my neighbor can practically unhinge her hip joints.

Similar physical differences are certainly present inside our bodies as well. One woman may have textbook anatomy, but her neighbor has a disconnected fallopian tube. Thankfully, malformations of the body due to

> ## "We are all made exactly alike, but with infinite differences."

injury or congenital development do not automatically mean infertility—in one rare case, a woman had eleven children before her doctors discovered she had a malformed uterus and only one ovary.[3] That's right: eleven children. In the cases where malformations are interfering with conception, endoscopy is a likely solution. Typically an outpatient procedure, endoscopy is a nearly noninvasive surgery that produces little scarring on the stomach or at the site of the surgical repair.

Polycystic Ovary Syndrome

Kristine's story accurately reflects the frustration 5–10 percent of all menstruating women feel when diagnosed with PCOS. It is a condition that is equal parts mystery and complexity. Doctors refer to polycystic ovary syndrome as *multispecialty*, meaning patients need not only a gynecologist but also an endocrinologist, dermatologist, and nutritionist to properly manage it. It affects a woman both on the outside and inside. Symptoms include:

- acne flare-ups coinciding with the menstrual cycle, resistant to topical treatments, and requiring hormone replacement for full control
- excessive facial hair in unusual areas, such as around the chin
- male-patterned hair loss
- thickening skin in creases, such as the neck, elbow, and behind the knee
- insulin-related symptoms, such as high blood sugar, fatigue, fatty liver, and anxiety
- irregular menstrual cycles.[4]

PCOS is a cyclical disease: insulin resistance can be a result of imbalanced hormones, but imbalanced hormones can cause insulin resistance. The most common and most effective therapy for fertility patients is breaking that cycle through weight loss, increased physical activity, and a whole-foods diet. Such lifestyle changes are important to any woman wanting to conceive, whether she has PCOS or not, and will be further explored in chapter 5.

"Try not to worry. It only makes things worse . . ."

It has been clinically proven that stress reduces an already-infertile couple's ability to conceive.[5] In a nutshell, stress naturally induces the body's fight-or-flight response, which raises hormone and protein levels in the blood. As our brains focus almost exclusively on physical survival, less-necessary processes (such as reproduction) are slowed down or stopped entirely.

When there are so many possible causes of infertility, fear and worry are natural reactions. A patient wants answers as soon as possible, so it is tempting to turn to the Internet. Thanks to medical websites, we have all become armchair physicians. Unfortunately the information at our fingertips tends to highlight the rare and worst-case scenarios. No matter

> **More effective than even quality medical treatment in balancing the body's stress response is a proper spiritual perspective.**

how much time we spend "researching" a condition online, no amount of anecdotal or even quality medical information will alleviate tension.

Instead of indulging our curiosities after an infertility diagnosis, we *patients* should practice *patience* and wait for the informed opinions of the medical professionals. I am not suggesting you be apathetic in advocating for your health. Make sure you are comfortable with your physicians and clinicians, ask them every question you can think of every time you see them, and trust them. Do your best to partner with a doctor who shares your value system. You may encounter life-threatening issues together as you and your husband attempt to conceive, and you are more likely to trust a practitioner with your worldview. If you ever find yourself doubting the care you're receiving, change doctors—don't become your own. A trusting relationship between a well-educated, well-liked doctor and an infertility patient is an effective way to manage fear during this uniquely stressful time.

More effective than even quality medical treatment in balancing the body's stress response is a proper spiritual perspective. Fear and worry are forms of bondage that take not only a physical toll on our lives, but a spiritual toll as well. The apostle Paul, in his final letter to Timothy, reminded his young disciple that "God did not give us a cowardly spirit but a powerful, loving, and disciplined spirit" (2 Tim. 1:7). God did not design us to stress out; He gave us naturally strong spirits. Paul wrote these words from his prison cell, where he awaited execution. What could be more stressful than that situation? He knew that Timothy would be afraid to "suffer for the good news" without his mentor, so Paul reassured him that God would protect him.

> God has *already* saved us and called us to [testify about our Lord]— not because of any good works we may have done, but because of His own intention and because eons and eons ago *(before time itself existed)*, He gave us this grace in Jesus the Anointed, *the Liberating King.* . . . I was appointed a preacher, emissary, and teacher of this message. This is exactly why I am suffering. But I am not ashamed because I know Him and I have put my trust in Him. And I am fully certain that He has the ability to protect what I have placed in His care until that day. (2 Tim. 1:9, 11–12)

We will discuss faith issues more completely in chapter 4, but until we get there, remember one thing: "He has the ability to protect what I have placed in His care until that day." Paul was placing himself, Timothy, and the amplification of the gospel in God's hands. He was releasing his own perceived control of the world and trusting God to take care of the plans He had made "eons ago." Infertility can put you in bondage to fear, worry, and stress; so when you feel those chains, place yourself in God's care. Trust Him and His plan for you and your future. Abandoning fear and embracing trust takes practice and patience—trust me!—but He is the best navigator of the stressors you encounter along the infertility journey.

Questions

1. How long after you married did you first feel pressured to start a family? How did you handle the questions?

2. What was your greatest fear as you started trying to conceive?

3. What causes you to worry? What could you do to minimize the negative effects of stress on your body and spirit?

4. What is your "spiritual perspective" on your infertility struggle? How does the Holy Spirit strengthen your naturally "powerful, loving, and disciplined spirit"?

"That Happened to So-and-So"

Understanding the prevalence of Infertility

Surely you've noticed: everyone knows someone who is struggling to have a child. Infertility, commonly defined as one year of unprotected intercourse that does not result in conception, occurs in approximately 15 percent of all American women aged fifteen to forty-four, according to a recent study.[1] That number does not seem very high, until you consider that not all of the seven thousand study participants were actively trying to get pregnant.

So what is the percentage of infertility among couples wanting to conceive? Determining a precise number is difficult because research and surveys can be conducted only on people who pursue medical help. It is impossible to know how many infertile people never seek medical advice due to high cost of treatment, embarrassment over the condition, or ignorance of the symptoms. Anecdotally it has been suggested to me by a reproductive endocrinologist that 38 percent of women between twenty-five and thirty-five wishing to conceive are infertile. Among that age demographic, infertility is literally epidemic.

"You aren't that infertile . . ."

In April 2005 my best friend, Melinda, and I were defending our final papers in a course entitled "Historiography in the Ancient Near East: The Arameans." (Exciting stuff, right?) She made the oh-so-scandalous mistake of saying something like, "Their buildings were a little bit unique." The professor stopped the class and leaned across the table, preparing to verbally attack Melinda. We could all see the explosion coming; I expected him to tear apart her point. Instead he roared at her, "It is impossible to be 'a little bit' unique. It's like being 'a little bit' pregnant. You either are pregnant or you aren't pregnant!" Point taken, but did he really need to stop her presentation for that? On the up side, I'm sure no one in that room—or on that floor of the building—ever made that grammatical error again.

Unlike pregnancy, which is indeed all-or-nothing, it is possible to be "a little bit" infertile. Within the medical community, three distinct conditions are lumped into the *infertility* category:

- *Subfertility* is any unwanted delay in conception that can result in pregnancy without medical intervention.

- *Primary infertility* is an inability to conceive with or without medical intervention.

- *Secondary infertility* is an inability to conceive again after any previous pregnancy, be it ectopic, miscarried, stillbirth, or live birth.

Most couples who have trouble conceiving quickly are actually *subfertile*—or "a little bit" infertile—but doctors commonly diagnose patients with either primary or secondary infertility before treatment begins. The degree to which someone is infertile is determined by medical history, physical examination, and hormone levels.

Michaela's Story

I never thought we'd have problems having children. Shortly after we married, Stephen and I decided we wanted to start a family, so we just did it. I got pregnant with Zachary on our first attempt, and I had no problems at all with the pregnancy. About a year and a half later, we decided to try for number two, and again I became pregnant immediately. Everything felt normal—then it wasn't.

My gynecologist acted as if a miscarriage is as normal for a woman as an annual exam is. When he gave me the news and I asked why it had happened and what we should do, he actually said to me, "This is just your first miscarriage," and refused to do any testing. To this day I don't know what caused the miscarriage. I understand that miscarriages are common for him; he must see these cases every day. But it wasn't normal for me. I needed compassion.

Because I was only eight weeks along when I miscarried, I hadn't told many people I was pregnant—just my mom and some friends. Mom couldn't relate to what I was going through, but she did her best to be supportive and sensitive. I didn't know if I should tell people about the miscarriage, especially since I hadn't confided my pregnancy to them; but once I shared, I realized so many were going through the same thing. At my church alone, four women had all suffered the same tragedy within weeks or even days of my miscarriage. There I found my compassion.

Of course Stephen was supportive, but he was aggrieved too. He didn't know how to handle the situation or me. I was asking so many questions: *Why would God do this? Do we try again? Do we risk experiencing this pain again?* Because of the miscarriage, we both realized that God is a huge factor in our family planning. Whereas before we just "did it" knowing *we* wanted a family, this

15

time we understood God has a will for this aspect of our lives. The miscarriage put reality in my face: He chose for us not to have that child. A year and a half later, I still don't understand why; I don't even know how to process that thought.

But God is faithful, even when I am doubting Him and confused about His plan for my family. The very next month I was pregnant with Jacob. I kept waiting to have a problem with him; I worried until the moment he arrived. It was nine months of misery made worse by

We don't know His plan, but we are going to trust God with our family and every aspect of our lives.

the fact that everyone was calling him Number Two. Intermingled with the extreme stress and latent joy of Jacob's pregnancy was the constant reminder that my real Number Two is in heaven.

I'd never noticed the prevalence of miscarriage until it happened to me, and I'm sad to admit that I have probably referred to someone's "Number Two" without consideration of what may have happened in her life. Before my miscarriage I would dismiss others' problems shortly after learning about them, but now that I have Jacob, I realize that longing for the lost child never goes away. Ironically, I find myself simultaneously carrying guilt about how easy pregnancy has been for me, relative to some of my friends. Three times in a row I got pregnant on our first try. I can't explain that either.

So what have Stephen and I learned from this pain? God is in control, and we must trust Him. With Jacob, I had to trust Him for my health and for Jacob's safe delivery. Now I have to trust His will is the best plan for the rest of my life. Will we have more kids? We're still debating that. We thought we'd be done after Jacob, but maybe not. I still worry about miscarriage, and I don't want to repeat that stress. But maybe God will have us adopt; maybe we'll have another biological child. We don't know His plan, but we are going to trust God with our family and every aspect of our lives.

"Fertility clinics are conveyor belts . . ."

I'll never forget the first appointment David and I had at a fertility clinic. We walked up to the entrance—ten-foot-tall double doors with a massive wooden overhang and a sign screaming (to us), "Enter here, all ye who are barren!" We felt the despair that permeated the place. We spent two hours in the doctor's office, though we only spent about ten minutes with her. In those ten minutes she told us our problems were common and gave us some copy-machine literature; then we left with a list of dates we had to return to the clinic for ultrasounds, injections, and intrauterine insemination. The doctor said that if three cycles of IUI failed, then David and I would have to find an additional $8,888 to begin our IVF (in vitro fertilization) treatments. This is what they did for all their patients. Several years later, we learned that if the clinic had taken my medical history and run one simple blood test that day, they would have known that IUI and IVF were unlikely to work for us.

Infertility care has not always been so cookie-cutter. When the first IVF-conceived baby was born in the United States in 1981, IVF was illegal in some states. Elizabeth Comeau's parents had to travel from their home in Massachusetts to Norfolk, Virginia, to conceive her as part of a medical trial. Their care was highly specialized to their needs, and their doctor, Howard Jones, has stayed in contact with the family. After naturally conceiving and giving birth to her own son in 2010, Mrs. Comeau reflected, "Our 2008 visit [to see Dr. Jones] was like a family trip, because Jones is more like a grandfather than a doctor to me. It was important to me that my husband and the man who perfected the technology to bring me into this world meet. I still get phone calls from Jones, now 99, on my birthday and Christmas—or during major life events—and we visit our 'family' in Norfolk whenever we can."[2]

Since Elizabeth Comeau's birth, IVF has become part of the American vernacular. Shortly before her birth, the U.S. federal government legalized IVF research and approved grants to fertility clinics. Thanks largely to those funds, private donations, media exposure, and advances in fertility science, there were 1 million IVF babies in the world and 450 IVF clinics

Twenty-three percent of fertility patients stop treatment too early due to emotional distress.

in the United States by 2004. Today, over 5 million babies have been born because of IVF and other reproductive technologies.[3]

Considering that approximately four hundred thousand American births are aided by fertility specialists each year, it is understandable that overloaded doctors may grow desensitized to their patients' emotions. It is understandable, but still hurtful. Thankfully the medical community itself has realized the need for a better bedside manner in infertility cases.

In September 2013, Dutch doctors concluded research on the quality of care, quality of life, and level of distress among patients in thirty-two fertility clinics. Recognizing that fertility patients experience unique physical and psychological burdens that may last for years, they recommended that physicians use a multifaceted approach to care that goes beyond treatment of physical symptoms to treatment of emotional and psychological issues during infertility procedures. It is hoped that treating patients holistically will improve fertility clinics' success rates. At the moment, 23 percent of fertility patients stop treatment too early due to emotional distress.[4]

"I've seen worse . . ."

Insensitivity is not unique to fertility clinicians. Within more than one community of women, I've heard conversations about child-bearing turn into a strange game of one-upmanship. There's competition on all sides. Ever heard a verbal competition between two women watching their toddlers play at the park? Maybe it sounded something like this:

"Darla was eleven pounds when she was born, and I didn't use any drugs during labor."

"I had a natural childbirth, too, but I did mine at home. The next time, you should try my doula. She had me walk around my house during the contractions to speed up my labor."

"There won't be a next time. We've decided our family is complete."

"Really? I would never tell God how many children He should give me."

"Well, at least my children won't feel neglected because they have so many siblings and never get one-on-one time with me."

What motivates such a hurtful conversation between friends who should be supporting each other? The coexisting feelings of pride and inadequacy. I'm very sad to say I've heard similar conversations between childless women:

"I just miscarried."

"We've been trying to have another baby for almost a year. I've just had my first appointment at the fertility clinic. Let me give you the number."

"Thanks, but we've been seeing a doctor for several months already. This was actually my second miscarriage."

"Really? I've had four."

"At least you have one at home already. That must make it easier to move forward."

"You're a mama too! Your baby is just in heaven."

So who is worse off? Who "won" the argument? I cringe just reading this conversation because I have truly been on the receiving end of most of those comments.

Because infertility seems common among people in their childbearing years, it is tempting to compare our circumstances to others' and make value judgments about our lives. We feel the need to justify our feelings to those around us, so when a friend goes through something we perceive to be worse than our own experiences, we try to ignore our own pain or maybe make it sound worse than it truly is to "fit in." (I suspect this may be exacerbated when doctors do not validate their patients' emotional distress.) In time, ignored emotions will manifest physically, and that can be dangerous. Each woman's journey is essential to her personal development and should not be compared to others'.[5]

Avoidance Coping

Every person copes with tragedy in a unique way. For most, coping begins passively. A woman bruised by infertility may

- avoid being with pregnant women or children;
- try to keep her feelings to herself;
- turn to a substitute activity to forget her heartache;
- hope a miracle will happen; or
- fantasize about how fertility treatments might turn out.

Such a passive strategy may work for a time. The problem is that as infertility treatments continue—possibly for years—passive coping isolates the patient from the rest of the world and forces her to suffer in silence.

Simply because of my age, I was surrounded by women getting pregnant at the same time I was enduring painful, ineffective treatments and miscarriages. Avoiding the world at first meant avoiding my pain, but soon I realized that I was making my entire existence about my personal tragedies. I would make decisions about where to go and what to do based on the likelihood of running into pregnant women or small children. One Christmas season I whipped into a close parking space at Target only to be smacked in the face by a Pregnant Mothers' Parking Only sign. That killed my holiday spirit. In a way, I was making my own situation worse by shutting out anyone who could share my burden and by letting so many insignificant situations rule my life.

Active Coping

When I finally followed my internist's instructions and began seeing a talk therapist, my world began to open up again. She gave me the tools I needed to process my own pain and reenter society. She guided me to the book *Boundaries*,[6] and she taught me to balance the physical, emotional, intellectual, and spiritual components of my life. Like mine, another woman's active coping mechanism may include

* accepting sympathy from someone;
* asking other childless people for advice;
* talking to someone about her emotions;
* thinking about alternative ways to become a parent;
* developing close relationships with other people's children;
* taking a break from trying to have a (or another) child; and
* pursuing a physically healthy lifestyle.

I don't think it's possible to dive into active coping the moment you discover you are infertile. When you are ready to understand the fact that your medical journey influences the course of your life—whether or not you have a child at the end of it—then it is time to start letting people in. I found comfort among my blood relatives, my church family, and a handful of truly caring medical professionals. Surround yourself with those who will support and encourage you, and be ready to laugh off those who don't. (If you ask me, laughter is the best way to deal with insensitive comments.)

"You remind me of Job . . ."

All of us have seasons in our lives that are particularly difficult. There may be times when your friends and loved ones compare you to the most downtrodden man of all time, Job.

Job became the unwitting object of a great debate in heaven. The Accuser, an angelic adversary of God, stood before His heavenly throne and suggested that humanity was devoted to God only when He gave them good things.

> **The Accuser:** *I won't argue with You that [Job] is pious,* but is all of this *believing in You and* honoring You for no reason? Haven't You encircled him with Your very own protection, and *not only him but* his entire household and all that he has? *Not only this, but* Your blessing accompanies whatever his hand touches, and see how his possessions have grown. *It is easy to be so pious in the face of such prosperity.* So now extend Your hand! Destroy all of these possessions of his, and he will certainly curse You, right to Your face.

> **Eternal One:** *I delegate this task to you.* His possessions are now in your hand. One thing, though: you are not to lay a finger on the man himself. *Job must not be touched.* (Job 1:9–12)

God allowed the Accuser to take everything away from Job: his possessions, his family, and his health. What follows in Job's story is his more-than-justified identity crisis, during which three of his oldest friends and one young eavesdropper attempted to diagnose the source of Job's sufferings. But all they ended up doing was making Job angry or even more depressed. None of them had an answer for why Job had suffered. Sound familiar?

God had to speak to Job Himself and remind the man that He was greater and more powerful than humanity would ever comprehend. That didn't exactly answer the question, why did Job suffer? But it did highlight the bigger picture: God knows what He is doing.

> **Job:** I know You can do everything;
>   nothing You do can be foiled *or frustrated.*
> *You asked,*
>   "Who is this that conceals counsel with *empty* words void of
>   knowledge?"
> *And now I see that* I spoke of—*but did not comprehend*—
>   *great* wonders that are beyond me. I didn't know.
> *You said,* "Hear Me now, and I will speak.
>   I'll be asking the questions, and you will supply the answers."
> Before I knew only what I had heard of You,
>   but now I have seen You.
> Therefore *I realize the truth:*
>   I disavow and mourn *all I have said*
>   and repent in dust and ash. (Job 42:1–6)

Because of his suffering, Job for the first time in his genuinely pious life was able to see God and understand His power. Job had spent years in mourning, listening to the intellectual arguments of the less-pious men around him and trying to figure out on his own why he had lost everything. In the end, the *why* didn't matter. It wasn't about the stuff. It wasn't about the suffering. It was about the outcome: Job had to learn that God is bigger than everything.

In the midst of suffering, it is easy to get down in the dust and ashes with Job and mourn. It's okay to be there; but when you are down there writhing with him, try to remember what Job learned: God is bigger than your pain. He hasn't explained to you why you are suffering, and just maybe that's because He wants you to focus on the bigger picture. Have confidence in the truth of who He is. He is your number-one supporter; He is the only "coping mechanism" that can move you beyond a life of survival to one of growth. Allow God to teach and to comfort you.

Questions

1. Are you surprised by the percentage of menstruating women who suffer with infertility? Why or why not?

2. Have you been bruised by the insensitivity of others? What happened, and how did you respond?

3. How have you learned to cope with the ups and downs of your medical journey? What can you do in the short term to feel better, and what do you want to change as you move forward?

4. What does God want to tell you about your suffering?

CHAPTER THREE

"Maybe You Aren't Doing It Right"

Facing Marital Pressures

Trying to get pregnant puts stress on the physical and emotional relationships in a marriage; but add to it fertility drugs, injectable hormones, feelings of inadequacy, and maybe even male infertility, and any marriage may suffer.

"Identify and address your fears . . ."

Pregnancy is a scary time for anyone. The woman may wonder, *Am I doing everything right? What is happening to my body? Will the birth be painful?* The man may worry, *How are we going to pay for this? What will happen to my free time? What will happen to our* alone *time?* Even if you've never had children, you've heard couples wonder about these exact questions. They are the topics of situation comedies, dramatic movies, and even morning radio chatter. Their sheer prevalence makes these fears easier to anticipate, process, and alleviate.

But not many people talk about the fears associated with *not* getting pregnant: *Can we afford treatments? Will the treatments hurt? Whose fault is this anyway? What will happen to us? Will we ever be happy again?* You won't hear these discussed by radio DJs in the car on your way to work, but these questions are common. They don't have immediate answers, and they certainly don't have right answers. All you can do at the beginning of the infertility process is tell your husband what you are afraid of, listen to his fears, and promise to see each other through the unknown. You are in this together.

Penny's Story

When I was a junior in college, my father sat our family down at Thanksgiving and told us he was gay. My parents had been married for twenty years. As you might imagine, this news affected my belief in marriage.

Years later when I was twenty-six and enjoying a successful career in engineering, my New England–based employer started sending me to South Carolina for months at a time. One morning I was minding my own business at the photocopier when a cute blond guy hit on me. For a woman working in a primarily male career field, this was not an unprecedented occurrence. But the difference this time was I was interested in him. Luke, the cute blond, surprised me, intrigued me, and soon won my heart.

About a year into our relationship, we hit the "hard stuff": he wanted marriage and kids; I didn't. Up until that point, we had avoided our differences of opinion, but as the relationship deepened and I considered making a permanent move to South Carolina to be with him, we had to come to a resolution. He wanted to get married; I wasn't sure I believed in marriage. He wanted "kids that are ours"; I was terrified of pregnancy. Yes, I was afraid of the pain associated with childbirth, but it was more than that. I was afraid of morning sickness, worried about having a "parasite" in my body, and wondering, *Where will all of my insides go?*

At that time I was already going to a therapist for help with other stressors in my life, so I brought up these topics too. The therapist helped me share my thoughts with Luke, and we realized we had time before he wanted to have kids. I loved him very much and didn't want to lose him.

A few years down the road, my feelings about marriage changed. Luke was so solid in his love for me and certain that we should be married, and before I knew it my reservations about marriage melted away and we married. The craziest part was, everything about it just felt right.

After about a year of being married, the topic of getting pregnant and having kids surfaced again. We talked and he re-shared his feelings that he wanted to have kids with me. I noticed how both of us had become more cuddly with our dogs and how I had a slight pang when we hung out with friends who had kids. I thought about all the scary, intimidating situations I'd overcome in my life; and I realized that once I was on the other side, they weren't as scary or bad as I had imagined. Ultimately I decided I didn't want to miss

Don't sacrifice the family you already have in an attempt to make a bigger one.

out on a huge life experience because of my fears. Plus I wasn't alone; I had the support and love of my husband.

After we talked some more, we decided to take a monthlong trip to Europe, then come home and start trying. At that point I had a whole new set of fears: What if I'd waited too long and we had trouble getting pregnant? (We were both over thirty.) What if we got pregnant immediately and our lives were turned upside down too quickly? (It takes me a while to adjust to change.)

As it turned out, neither fear played out. It took a few months to get pregnant, and I've had a pleasant pregnancy. There wasn't any morning sickness, and my insides all still seem to be in there somewhere. Now that I'm pregnant, am I still freaked out? Yes, of course! But Luke and I have already learned that love can overcome anything. Working through different issues over the years has made our marriage relationship strong and our commitment to our family sure.

"You may not be the problem . . ."

Ladies, if you think infertility clinics are uncomfortable for you, imagine how your husband feels. We have the benefit (if you want to call it that) of experience in gynecological settings. We have annual exams, regularly talk about our cycles with doctors, and are familiar with some of those ridiculously cold and pointy tools they use. This stuff is alien to men. How many husbands are so embarrassed by it all that they refuse to purchase feminine products for their wives at the local drugstore? (Seriously, what check-out girl is going to think he's buying them for himself?)

He's already freaked out by the stories you tell him about your gynecologist—let alone your first appointment with a fertility specialist—and then you slap him with, "You have to go to a urologist before they'll do any more testing on me." He doesn't hear, "urologist." He hears, "prostate exam." Assuming he's under age fifty and hasn't had medical issues in the past, your husband is about as excited for his first prostate exam as you were for your first annual pap smear. And what does he have to do after his physical exam at the urologist's office? Leave a "deposit." We aren't talking about co-pays here.

Male-Factor Infertility

Although the testing process may feel alien and lonely for men, male-factor infertility is not unusual. Studies show that 20 percent of diagnosed infertile couples have only male-factor infertility, and another 35 percent of diagnosed infertile couples have both male- and female-factor infertility.[1] When he walks into a fertility clinic, odds are the men he sees there are having issues themselves. (But don't expect your husband to cozy up beside his neighbor and swap stories about the urologist.)

Just as they do for women, the potential sources of male infertility range widely. The initial testing stages are also the same: taking a medical and social history, performing a physical exam, and testing hormone levels in the blood. Men have the additional step of the semen analysis. This is arguably the most informative piece of a doctor's diagnosis. Semen analyses test

- the quantity of sperm;
- the motility of the sperm;
- the morphology (shape) of the sperm;
- the agglutination (stuck-togetherness) of the sperm;
- the liquefaction of semen; and
- the pH of the semen.

Unfortunately there is little that can be done to change the quality of semen if it is judged substandard. There is no male fertility drug out there that can magically improve things (although some doctors are prescribing Clomid in hopes of increasing the number of sperm, with mixed results[2]).

As with everything in life, diet and exercise are a man's best hope of improving his fertility. If he loses weight and avoids artificial hormones in food, toiletries, and household products, his hormones can naturally balance. If he stops consuming caffeine and alcohol, eats a nutritious diet, and consumes the right vitamins and minerals, his semen quality may improve. If these concepts are anathema to him, remind your husband that these are healthy habits he would probably want to pass on to his children. These changes will definitely improve his quality of life, may help you get pregnant, and are examples of good behavior to those around him.

Male Psychology

Healthy diets and regular exercise naturally elevate anyone's mood. Considering the stress your husband is certain to encounter during testing and treatment, every positive lifestyle change will help him. You can expect that "men who perceive themselves to be the sole contributor to the couple's infertility feel less in control of their lives, less able to meet their goals, and more personally responsible for their fertility problems. Furthermore, this group of men has lower sexual satisfaction, more feelings of sexual failure, and less enjoyment of sexual activity."[3] A diagnosis of infertility will affect every aspect of his life—just as it does yours. Recognize his struggles, face your challenges together, and safeguard your marriage.

"Infertility destroyed my marriage . . ."

Billy Crystal is the best host the Academy Awards has ever hired. He's funny without being crude, and that typically extends to his movies. I recently learned that he is insanely in love with his wife of forty-three years,[4] so that also makes him the most attractive actor in Hollywood. Back in 1995 he and Debra Winger starred in *Forget Paris*, the story of a couple named Mickey and Ellen who struggles to make their marriage work in spite of demanding jobs, long-distance living, and—you guessed it—infertility.

Mickey and Ellen have been doing rounds of IVF for two years when their close friends have a baby. Standing at the window to the hospital nursery, staring longingly at the dozens of newborns, they decide to take a break.

Ellen: I'm tired.

Mickey: Then let's go home.

Ellen: I mean, I'm tired of the whole thing. I want to stop.

Mickey: Do you want to adopt?

Ellen: I don't know. I just want some time not to have to think about it for a while.

By then, the damage had been done to their relationship. Ellen takes a promotion that moves her to Paris, and the couple separates.[5]

The movie is funny and warm—you'll laugh your head off at the scene where Billy Crystal has to engage a police escort to get his "deposit" to the fertility clinic in the middle of stand-still traffic. But it is also poignant. No specific studies have been published giving the rate of divorce among infertility patients, but common sense tells us that couples who endure infertility treatment are more likely to divorce.[6] Emotions are running high, and it is easy for couples to lose sight of each other as they focus on the goal of having a child. The tragedy in this scenario is the break-up of the husband and wife, not the failed attempts at a successful pregnancy.

As couples face infertility, they must remember that marriage covenants are unbreakable. Genesis tells us that "a man leaves his father and his mother, and is united with his wife; and the two become one flesh" (2:24). Once your relationship is consummated, you are one person. You cannot be separated. But just as you did not promise to stay married only if you had children, God didn't gift married people with sex for the sole purpose of procreation. It is supposed to be an intimate time that strengthens the bond between you and your spouse. (If you doubt me on this, read the Song of Songs before turning off the light tonight!)

Fertility treatments can strip love and romance from the bedroom. Our bodies were not made to run on artificial hormone injections, and our libidos don't respond just because it is Day 10 on your cycle-charting calendar. It may be necessary to stop or pause treatment in order to save your marriage (and your sanity). Make a conscious effort to let your spouse know that sex isn't goal-oriented; it is still about the two of you. You want to be with him whether or not your time together is clinically (re)productive.

Consider seeking professional help as soon as you are diagnosed; your doctors and fertility clinicians will be able to recommend psychiatrists, psychologists, and counselors whose practices fit your needs and who can give you tools to cope. I found that talk therapy was helpful, though David never went with me. It annoyed me at the time, but I now realize that things worked out anyway. When I would come home and talk to him after an appointment, I was confident in what I said and what I felt because I'd already processed my emotions with a professional. If I could talk to him rationally, then we could better avoid arguments and hurt feelings. Most important, we could move forward as a couple.

For a list of books David and I used for marriage support, see the Suggested Resources section beginning on page 132.

David's Story

When we first married and Amanda would ask me how many kids I wanted us to have, I'd answer, "However many God gives us." I knew this terrified my only-child wife on some level (which was part of the fun in saying it), but I truly meant it. I didn't have any grand plans for the size of our family or how it would function. I did, however, assume God would give us at least a couple of kids. I am the oldest of four siblings; big families are normal to me. When we first realized that getting and staying pregnant wasn't going to be as easy for us as it seemed to be for everyone around us, I simply didn't know how to react.

There is nothing comfortable about the infertility process for a man. To begin with, your bedroom life suddenly becomes news for a bunch of doctors and nurses you've only just met. And most of them are other women. We husbands have been trained *not* to talk about what happens behind our closed doors, so this just feels wrong. Then once those strangers have dissected your relationship, they start treating your wife (who is slowly going insane because of all the junk they are pumping into her) and turn you into a not-so-glorified sperm donor.

The "deposit" part was the worst for me. First of all, when you are a man walking into a fertility clinic, you know that everyone else knows why you are there. You don't fist-bump the guy sitting just as uncomfortably as you in the chair next to yours; you do your best to forget that you, too, know why *he* is there. You find yourself clocking exactly how long each man spends in that room before you are called. You worry that if you're too fast, then the doctors will think you have a problem; you worry that if you're too slow, you'll have a line of people staring at you when you reemerge. Finally, when you are called out of the waiting room, you are put in a windowless room (by a female nurse who also knows why you are there) with pornography. Pornography is bad. Amanda would never dream of letting me buy even a *Maxim* magazine (and I would never dream of doing so). Husbands aren't supposed to look at pornography . . . unless they are trying to get their wives pregnant? What kind of sense does that make?

When something makes me uncomfortable, I want to fix the problem. When I can't fix a problem immediately, I get frustrated and shut out the problem and everyone associated with it. That may be a stereotypical male response, but it became a stereotype for a reason. Amanda does the exact opposite. She embraces a problem and dwells on it. She lets it take over her life until it is solved. What did this look like in our home? Amanda standing in the shower, crying her eyes out every night because she is tired of counting days and popping pills. Me sitting on the couch, flipping through channels because *The Simpsons* is great way to escape my memories of that "deposit" room.

Six years after we started all this mess, I had a kind of breakthrough. Actually, God hit me over the head with the proverbial frying pan. One Sunday the youth director at our church, A. J. Farley, delivered a message dissecting Job 2. He made the point that when Christians "comfort" one another, we have the tendency to "simply dismiss [the grieving person] with a platitude or, worse yet, a passage of scripture in the way that Job's friends attempted to do." We act as if spouting Romans 8:28 will fix everything, and then we "walk away, leaving that brother or sister in an intensified pain."[7] I realized I'd been doing this to Amanda.

I apologized to her as soon as A. J.'s sermon was finished and before we took Communion. We then went home, opened a bottle of wine, and talked for hours about what we needed from each other outside all the doctors' appointments and prescription refills. Amanda explained to me (probably for the millionth time) that she didn't need me to "be a man" in the archaic sense; I had thought I was being strong for her, but I was only making her feel weak. She needed to know that I was hurting as much as she was; I had thought crying with her would deepen her depression, but it would have justified her pain.

If I could change anything that happened during those years of treatment, it would be how I responded to my wife and how long it took me to change that. I wish I had been someone she could pour out her heart to, instead of someone she felt judged by. This is what God taught me through our struggles, and I know I am blessed that He could use the pain to teach us more about each other and bring us closer together. If we had never encountered life-altering tragedy, we might not have ever learned how the other really ticks. Amanda has a sensitive soul—that's one of the many things I love about her—and deep down, I do too. I now know I need to let her see it more often.

"Put your marriage first . . ."

There is no story of male infertility in the Bible. Whenever conception was delayed, the woman was labeled as barren. But we see in Elkanah, the father of the Old Testament prophet Samuel, how a husband should respond to his wife when children don't come (regardless of who is infertile). He was a man of few words, but those words were full of love. Just as David wanted to do for us, Elkanah tried to solve the problem for Hannah.

> On the days he made a sacrifice, Elkanah would share a portion *of his offering* with his wife Peninnah and all her children, but he offered a double portion *of sacrificial meat* for Hannah because he loved her even though the Eternal One had not given her children. . . . *As she often did,* Hannah wept and refused to eat.
>
> **Elkanah** (*seeing Hannah's despair*): Why are you crying and not eating? Why are you so sad, *Hannah?* Don't I love you more than any 10 sons could? (1 Sam. 1:4–5, 7–8)

He loved her. He wanted her to love him. Their relationship was more important to him than having children.

The New Testament requires husbands to love their wives (Eph. 5:25–33), but in our post-patriarchal society, most men don't have to be commanded to do so. We marry for love, not for position or progeny. Just because your husband doesn't express his love for you in the way that you express your love for him doesn't mean he has stopped loving you. Look for the little things he says and does. He probably won't be making a special sacrifice at the temple on your behalf, but he might give you more attention and pay you more compliments. Those small changes in his behavior will show you his heart and may indicate how he is silently sharing your pain.

Infertility is no one's fault, and it is just as painful for men as it is for women, although they usually do not express it as we do. Talk to your spouse. Share your heart, and do your best to discover what is inside his. It may take time, but communication will strengthen your marriage whether you have children or not. Your husband is your greatest ally in this. Listen to his wisdom. He may be seeing things more clearly because he isn't hyped up on hormones (be they artificial or natural). Just you and your husband constitute a family. Don't sacrifice the family you already have in an attempt to make a bigger one.

Questions

1. When you married, did you and your husband see eye to eye on family planning? If not, how did you resolve your differences?

2. What are your fears about starting a family? What are your husband's fears? How can you make each other feel secure as you plan your family?

3. Have you specifically asked your husband how he feels about your struggle to have children? If he has a medical problem, have you convinced him that you do not hold him responsible for the delay in growing your family?

4. Are you putting your husband's well-being ahead of your desire to have children? Do you need to make significant changes to your priorities and put your marriage first? If so, how will you do that?

CHAPTER FOUR

"All of the Matriarchs Were Infertile"

Questioning Your Faith

My elder said it, my best friend said it, and—to her absolute horror today—my mother said it. Before I struggled with infertility, I have no doubt that I cavalierly said it to some of my friends, too: "Sarah was ninety years old before she had Isaac." That seems to be the reaction you get whenever you tell your Christian friends that you're having trouble getting pregnant. To be fair, there is nothing anyone can say to make you feel better. All your loved ones want to do is bolster your faith by reminding you that you're in good company, that the heroines of our faith had the same heartache you do.

"Pray as Hannah did . . ."

When troubles come, it is tempting to open up the Bible and search for an example of someone who had the exact problem you have. That's not necessarily a bad strategy, but it often ignores the context of the biblical character's pain and leaves you with an incorrect prescription for your own healing. The Bible is not a medical textbook like *Gray's Anatomy*;

you won't find a diagram of your pain inside it. You will find stories that teach you about God's character.

Let's say hello to everyone's favorite barren women: Sarah and Hannah.

Sarah: "God has graced me with the gift of laughter!" (Gen. 21:6).

There once lived a rich old woman named Sarah. She and her husband, a trader named Abraham, were raising an adopted son named Ishmael, who would one day be the sole heir to Abraham's significant fortune. Ishmael was adored by his father, spending day after day with him, learning how to run the family business.

One particularly hot afternoon, Sarah was in her tent, just trying to stay cool. All of the servants were away from the camp, resting under trees, as was usual during the heat of the day. Drifting off to sleep, Sarah was startled when her frantic husband burst into the tent with an unusual demand: "Make some bread! Now!"

Just as abruptly he was gone.

Abraham had acquired great wealth in the last decades, so it had been a while since Sarah had made bread—and she'd certainly never made it

When troubles come, it is tempting to open up the Bible and search for an example of someone who had the exact problem you have.

at high noon. Her maidservants baked the bread in the mornings, when it was cooler; the oven would be cold now.

Curious as to what had agitated her husband, Sarah found herself standing behind the entrance flap of her tent. She could see that Abraham was providing the ingredients of an impressive feast for three strangers who had joined him under Abraham's favorite shade tree.

With all of their servants on siesta, ninety-nine-year-old Abraham was doing all the work. That sight alone was enough to amuse Sarah, but what she heard next nearly made her laugh out loud. One of the strangers announced to Abraham that she, an eighty-nine-year-old, postmenopausal woman, would give birth to a son in the next year. Not only was she beyond barren, but she and Abraham hadn't even enjoyed marital relations in quite a while. Clearly the sun's heat had baked this man's brain!

Suddenly she could feel the man's eyes burning a hole through the tent flap. "Is anything too hard for the Lord?" he asked.

She instinctively stepped back from the entrance, quietly denying her laughter and fearfully wondering how he had heard a noise she'd never made.

But the man answered her aloud again: "No, but you did laugh."

This must be God.

Several months later, Sarah's suspicions about the man's identity were confirmed. She was pregnant, and indeed, she would deliver a child within a year of the traveler's pronouncement. Only God could do this.

As soon as she delivered her son, Abraham named him Isaac, which means "he laughs." Sarah always knew Abraham had a sense of humor, and his choice of Isaac's name proved it. Not only had she laughed at the seemingly impossible news of her coming pregnancy, but Sarah knew that her reaction had made God laugh as well. She had been foolish to doubt the abilities of the one true God, but He had been faithful to her and given Sarah her heart's greatest desire: a son of her very own.

Hannah: "The Eternal remembered her petition; and in the new year, Hannah became pregnant" (1 Sam. 1:19–20).

There once was a charming woman named Hannah. She lived with her husband, Elkanah, in the foothills of Ephraim, about ten miles west of the Mediterranean Sea and about ten miles east of the city of Shiloh. They shared a comfortable, middle-class life. Elkanah was a pious man and loved Hannah dearly, but no matter how hard they tried, she could not give birth to an heir.

Elkanah did what he thought he had to do to make sure his family would survive: he married a second wife. Peninnah lived up to her name; she was indeed richly fertile. She gave Elkanah countless sons and daughters—and she gave Hannah tons of problems.

Every year the entire family would hike into the mountains on a special pilgrimage to the city of Shiloh. There the ark of the covenant was

Because of her journey to the tent in Shiloh, when she asked God to give her a child, Hannah had a deeper understanding of who God was.

resting, so Elkanah made a peace offering to the Eternal One on behalf of each member of his immediate family. Because a proper peace offering constituted the breast, right thigh, and fat of an animal, Elkanah had to slaughter one animal for each of his relatives. This took a lot of time, and while he was away from their camp, Peninnah would taunt Hannah. Knowing this was Peninnah's habit, Elkanah would make an extra offering on behalf of his beloved Hannah. He hated to see her in tears.

When he returned to the camp, the family would boil and eat the remaining meat, which was of course a great feast. It was supposed to be a time of celebration and thanksgiving, but Hannah was always so upset by Peninnah's attitude that she would cry and refuse to eat. Her fasting was tantamount to a rejection of the blessings, and Elkanah could never understand why his love and sacrifices on her behalf were not enough to make her happy. No matter how hard he tried to please her, Hannah would never be happy without a baby of her own.

One year Hannah changed her routine. It was the day after the family had feasted, and she went to the tent covering the ark of the covenant herself to make a request of the Eternal One. Hannah could not get as close to the ark as her husband or any of the priests could; she had to stay outside of the tent to pray, where it may not have been entirely clear to passersby what she was doing.

As she prayed silently and cried her eyes out, Hannah was being watched by Eli the priest. He thought she was drunk and chastised her: "How long are you going to continue drinking, *making a spectacle of yourself? Stop drinking wine, and sober up!*" (1 Sam. 1:14).

Hannah explained to him that she was not drunk. Her somewhat unusual public behavior was the result of the "wounded spirit" (v. 15) she'd carried for many years, and she'd come to ask the Eternal One to heal her by giving her a much-longed-for son. She was promising to give the boy over to God's service and to raise him in the strictest way possible—as a Nazirite who would never cut his hair or drink alcohol (ironic, since Eli thought she'd had some wine herself!).

Eli the priest seconded her request to God, and Hannah then returned to her family's camp, hopeful that she would now be blessed with a son. She was finally able to eat; thankfully the leftovers from the sacrifice were still good. The next morning the family worshiped the Eternal One, one last time before returning home.

Back in Ephraim where they could be comfortable in their own tent, Elkanah and Hannah slept together. The Eternal One remembered her prayer, and she became pregnant with a son within a few months. When the boy was born, Elkanah allowed Hannah to name him Samuel, which means "his name is God." Because of her journey to the tent in Shiloh, when she asked God to give her a child, Hannah had a deeper understanding of who God was. She could see His grace reflected in her tiny baby's smile.

What do Sarah and Hannah (and Rebekah and Rachel and other no-longer-barren women of the Bible) have in common? God blessed them with children. And that's great. In most cases it was miraculous! God looked down from heaven, saw their struggles, loved them, and blessed them with children. Sons, in fact. They got the happiest of endings in the time it takes to read less than one chapter of scripture. This is inspiring, right? This is why our loved ones reference them so readily.

A few months into your journey, you may take the encouragement as just that. You try to remind yourself that none of the matriarchs knew a successful pregnancy would be the outcome while they were in the midst of their monthly struggles. You think, *If I can have enough faith, God will bless me with a child too.* Maybe you pull out 1 Samuel 1 and read Hannah's prayer to God. Maybe you pray it yourself, every night, for weeks and months. You promise to raise your little one as a Nazirite, thinking there's no way you can keep from cutting his hair for his entire life and knowing she'll probably encounter alcohol by the time she gets out of college. That's the moment it dawns on you: *I'm already lying to God about my kid. I'm not good enough to be a mother.* In that moment remember: those matriarchs didn't have perfect faith either. God used their years of infertility to bring them closer to Him. Their struggles were, for their characters, less about having a baby and more about encountering God.

Rebecca's Story

Luke and I had been married for three years when we decided to have a baby. Within a month of making the decision, I was pregnant. We were both so excited. We told people right away, and at eight weeks the ultrasound showed a healthy heart and zero complications.

At ten weeks, I started spotting. There was a subchorionic hemorrhage on the placenta, but the doctors said not to worry because those are typically benign.

The bleeding stopped until the next week, when I awoke in the middle of the night to heavy bleeding. We called the emergency doctor and scheduled ultrasounds for the next morning. We discovered that the baby's body was there, but there was no heartbeat. The baby's growth had stopped at eight and a half weeks.

I elected to have the D and C immediately and was admitted to the hospital. My doctor was kind and compassionate. He sat on the corner of the hospital bed and prayed with me before the procedure.

The next thing I remember is waking up in recovery and knowing that I wanted to go back to sleep and never wake up. I went

> ### God's providence seems "great" when you're going through a great time, but it is much more confusing when you are not.

home and went to bed. I don't remember much else from the days immediately following my loss.

In the next months, I became angry and depressed. I wasn't me. I desperately wanted to experience the joy of pregnancy and motherhood, and I struggled to move on from the pain of losing our first baby.

After five months of trying, I was pregnant again. This time I was careful to do everything I was supposed to do, but at six weeks, I miscarried again and spiraled into darkness. I was crying all the time. Luke was heartbroken, too, and tried to comfort me, but all he could do was hold me while I cried.

About that time, our pastor began a sermon series about God's providence. I kept waiting for him to say, "God chose for your babies to die." Of course he didn't. He talked about how Joseph's life was guided by God, even when he was enslaved, wrongly accused, and imprisoned; so does that mean God guided this? I still don't know the answer to that question. I don't know if He divined the miscarriages. God's providence seems "great" when you're going through a great time, but it is much more confusing when you are not. This was not a great time.

I knew something had to change when I learned that a close friend had an accidental pregnancy, and I cried tears of anger, jealousy, and grief. That reaction wasn't me. I knew I shouldn't hate other people's joy, but I did. The next day, I threw my hands in the air and laid it all before God. "I don't like this situation, and I don't

I told Him, "Show me Your plans, and that's what we'll do."

like me. But I don't know how to stop it. I don't want to live like this, but it's not within my power to change things."

God changed things. In that moment and in the following weeks, the Holy Spirit gave me unexplainable joy and peace. I knew God in a way that I'd never known Him before. He truly did lift me out of darkness and put me in light. The circumstances hadn't changed; He was the only explanation. My anger went away, and submission was in my heart. There was still sadness, but I realized I was mourning my plans. I told Him, "Show me Your plans, and that's what we'll do."

That evening we cleared out the room where the baby stuff had been and put it all away. We didn't try not to get pregnant, but we didn't try to either. Luke began reading scripture over us daily in our home. It wasn't like flipping a switch: Satan was still attacking, trying to pull me back. But I knew God was sufficient. He provided all that I needed then. I truly experienced Jesus as my Savior.

Six weeks later we got pregnant. I fought fear. Hard. I'm not sure I took a breath until after the first trimester. I was fearful until I held her. Even after she was born, I was waiting for the next bad thing to happen; but He pushed us toward obedience and trust. We had a precious, teeny-tiny little girl. I thought, *That's it. I'm fixed now.*

My Annie was nearly two when we got pregnant again. I was surprised when I almost immediately miscarried. Because we had moved from Georgia to Virginia, I had a new doctor, who wanted to do some medical testing this time. I told her, "I've done this before. I don't have time to deal with it now. Let's schedule something next week." This time I was a mommy, so I just tucked the pain away because I had someone to take care of.

When I had a fourth miscarriage soon thereafter, I had to deal with my emotions. Each time I approached God in worship, I would cry. I could hide from people but not from God. There was no anger now; God had truly changed me before Annie was born. This time I clung tightly to Him instead of pushing Him away.

I was referred to a fertility specialist. As the appointment approached, Luke and I began praying, "Lord, this is it. This is Your chance for a miracle. You can do this now, and we will proclaim this is Your miracle. No doctor can take credit. If You don't, then that's okay." A month before the appointment I had a positive pregnancy test, and nine months later we again had a very tiny but very healthy baby. Kaylie is another miracle.

Recently I've come to a place where I can give thanks for the heartache. I now know God in a new way as my comforter, my peace, and my joy; and I know my husband as my partner through the good and the bad. I am thankful for the way God used our tragedies to grow our family, both literally and spiritually.

"Pray as Anna did . . ."

The next time someone tells you about Sarah or Hannah, try to remember that response is coming from a place of love. Then smile tolerantly and forget it! The Bible was not written by women. If it had been, then we'd know more about these women's day-to-day struggles and not go straight to the resolutions of their stories. The matriarchs—I'll admit it—are minor characters in God's redemptive story. The miracles of their pregnancies have more to do with the babies they had than the women they were. As a result, their stories don't offer us modern fertility patients very much help.

The most inspiring woman in the Bible, to me, is granted three verses of scripture. Anna was the wife of a temple priest, and she did not have children. She went to the temple courtyard every day, and she prayed. Because of her faithfulness, God promised she'd see the Christ child before she died. At eighty-four, Anna was doing her habitual morning prayer when Mary and Joseph walked in with eight-day-old Jesus. She held the baby, and she blessed him. After that we assume she died. That's all we know!

> At that very moment, an elderly woman named Anna stepped forward. Anna was a prophetess, the daughter of Phanuel, of the tribe of Asher. She had been married for seven years *before her husband died* and a widow to her current age of 84 years. She was *deeply devoted to the Lord*, constantly in the temple, fasting and praying. When she approached *Mary, Joseph, and Jesus*, she began speaking out thanks to God, and she continued spreading the word about Jesus to all those who shared her hope for the rescue of Jerusalem. (Luke 2:36–38)

Just like the matriarchs', Anna's story isn't about Anna. Luke didn't put it there so infertile women could identify with her. Her story is in the gospel because she identified Jesus as the Messiah. The fact that she was childless is ancillary. I wish I knew more about her. I wish I knew how she survived month after month of disappointment. I wonder if she was ever pregnant. Did she have a miscarriage? Did she have a baby and then lose him or her to illness?

Anna teaches us something very important. Her three verses of scripture prove that a child is not a reward for a woman's faithfulness to God. Meeting God face-to-face is the reward. As we struggle with our bodies and our faiths, it helps to keep a kingdom perspective on our lives. We are to remain faithful to God with the confident hope that we literally will meet Him face-to-face, be it in heaven or when Jesus returns. Until that day, we still have the opportunity to meet God every day when we pray. It is not the primary point of the scripture or the explicit purpose of Anna's character in the story, but I like to think the Holy Spirit slipped the detail in there to give me hope when I needed it most.

"Pray as God wants you to pray . . ."

Stroll through your local bookstore, and you'll find quite a few books written for women who are struggling to have children. They largely fall into two categories: self-help and (what I like to call) self-helpless.

The Self-Help Approach

Even if you haven't picked up one of these gems in the Health and Wellness aisle, I bet you've done a little Internet research looking for a quick fix to infertility. The idea is that you change something physical in your life—such as your sleeping position or your consumption of avocados—and you will magically get pregnant. These books tend to have fun titles, like *Charting the Full Moon: Pregnancy on the Universe's Cycle* or *The Tao of Baby Making: Confucius and the Buddha Never Had Wives with Fertility Issues* or *Mandrakes and You: Why One Ancient Fruit Is All It Takes to Heal Your Dusty Uterus.* (I may have made those up, but you get the point.)

I am not one to minimize the importance of a healthy lifestyle—I've devoted chapter 5 to it—but quantifiably successful use of alternative treatments is unsubstantiated.[1] As I said in chapter 2, I am not suggesting you be apathetic about your own health care; do as much research as will make you comfortable and give you confidence in your physician. If you want to up your consumption of guacamole, that's your prerogative. But once you know you have the best medical care, stop relying on alternatives. Searching for answers when your physician has already supplied them will only make you crazy, and "crazy" raises your stress level and makes it even harder to achieve and sustain a healthy pregnancy.

The Self-Helpless Approach

Failing an "easy" pseudo-medical solution, we leave the Health aisle and venture into the Religion aisle. Devotional books for the infertile are abundant, but most of them come to the same conclusion: if you have enough faith, then God will give you children. That may not be the intended message, but it's the one that comes across.

We like to say we trust God with the big and the little things, but it is difficult to practice that mantra and eliminate worry from our lives. I like that word, *practice*. We don't just have faith; we practice it. Just because we have doubts or fears in this time or in that place, and just because God

A child is not a reward for a woman's faithfulness to God. Meeting God face-to-face is the reward.

doesn't grant our wishes, doesn't mean we are devoid of faith. Faith, which is bestowed by the Holy Spirit, may be challenged by trials that give us the opportunity to practice trusting God and understand Him better. It is hard to keep that perspective when you are in the thick of your fertility battle—or any battle—but if God didn't choose to work in ways we never would, then would we recognize Him? Would we have a need for faith?

Let's discuss that word: *faith*. I've spent most of my life thinking faith is something I must manufacture myself. I suspect this comes from being part of a Christian culture that tends to love making its own rules, such as "Don't drink" and "Don't dance." No matter how strongly I believe that grace is what saves me from my sins, I want control. I want to be God. That was humanity's first sin, and it is at the root of every one of mine. If I make for myself a list of rules to follow, then I create the illusion (or rather, delusion) that I am in control of my salvation. That is especially attractive to a type-A control freak such as I, but it resonates with every human because none of us want to answer to anyone—not even God. We want to be our own bosses at work, at home, and even at church.

I can't manufacture my salvation, and I can't manufacture faith either. There are no rules—scriptural or otherwise—for how to produce more faith, because it is a gift given by God (much like grace) to those of us who "have chosen to walk with the Spirit, . . . each step in perfect sync with God's Spirit" (Gal. 5:25). This means living our lives with one purpose: furthering God's will.

We don't create faith, and we don't determine how much of it we have. However, we are not helpless when it comes to understanding God's will. Contrary to popular belief, God does not have six billion wills for the six billion people on this planet. Whether or not you have a baby is not God's will. He has one will: humanity's reconciliation with Him. It is when you adopt His one will as your one will that faith grows.

Understand that embracing His will means releasing your own designs on your personal future. But it doesn't mean you're just another number in God's congregation. God has an individual plan for your life that is specifically designed to further His will. That plan may or may not involve you being a parent, but it certainly will bring you the greatest joy imaginable as you come face-to-face with God.

Questions

1. What conversations or events have caused you to question your faith?

2. Is there a Bible character with whose faith journey you closely identify?

3. What crazy fertility "cures" have you read about, considered, or even tried? How did they make you feel?

4. Have you confused God's *will* with God's *plan* for your life? Are you willing to release your own desires to be a part of His greater work of reconciling the world to Himself?

CHAPTER FIVE

"Take Better Care of Yourself"

Putting Your Body First

Eat better and exercise more: that is the preventative solution for most diseases and disorders, infertility included. A lot of women think about what they put in their bodies after they become pregnant because they are focused on the health of the child, but your lifestyle while trying to conceive can determine whether or not you get to carry that child at all. Everything works together—mind, body, spirit, and emotions—so an imbalance in one area can make conception difficult. Most women are used to putting themselves last, but if we want to have a baby to sacrifice our time for in the future, we need to be a little selfish now.

"If you can't afford organic, then don't eat meat . . ."

According to the USDA, a child will cost a family nearly $250,000 to raise from birth to age eighteen.[1] In an economy where a lot of college graduates can't find jobs in their fields, wages are dropping, and prices are rising, budgeting is necessary for all families, especially those just starting their married lives who are most likely to procreate. It is tempting to cut out boring things, such as fresh fruits and vegetables, so we can keep our entertainment systems, vacations, and even pets. Before we start a family, we need to get all of our priorities straight, starting with our bodies.

I know you've heard it said, "Don't eat anything your grandmother wouldn't recognize," and, "Only shop the perimeter of your grocery store." When David and I started trying to conceive, I had to reconcile those say-

Your lifestyle while trying to conceive can determine whether or not you get to carry a child at all.

ings with my by-then-engrained Weight Watchers lifestyle. We had figured out how to work the Points system: every Sunday was chili dog and french fry night, thanks to fat-free buns, fat-free (and David would add, *squeaky*) hot dogs, fat-free sour cream, fat-free shredded cheddar, exactly twenty-one fries baked in the oven, and diet soda. We reached our goal weights, but were we healthy? Apparently not.

At my first meeting with our second fertility specialist, the doctor said we needed to make significant lifestyle changes not because we were overweight, but because both of us were estrogen dominant. Yes, my furry bear of a husband, whose thick mane of black hair my balding daddy gazes at jealously, was estrogen dominant. What was to be our guiding rule for these lifestyle changes? "Do your best *never* to shop at a grocery store. But don't get obsessed about it." Yeah, right. But my doctor knew what he was talking about. We followed his advice as best we could, and our hormones (mostly) balanced themselves in a matter of months.

One reason women and men all over the industrialized world are estrogen dominant is their consumption of animal products. Just when the news was talking about milk prices going up by a dollar per gallon,

David and I were leapfrogging to organic milk, a whopping five dollars per *half* gallon. Chicken went from three nights per week to once per month because we couldn't afford the organic stuff. Some hunter friends killed deer for us. We bought half of a grass-fed, pasture-raised cow, and no, we did not keep it in the backyard. (You'd be amazed how many people asked me that.)

My grandfather was a little offended when he found out we were making these changes. He was a dairy farmer for most of his adult life, selling his milk to the once-prolific brand, Sealtest. Just before he retired, innovation began impacting the food industry. The milking machine was revolutionary, allowing him to have a life outside the barn and off the milking stool. From his perspective, technology in the food industry was a good thing, and I was besmirching his livelihood by avoiding major brands. In fact, I was trying to find milk like what he used to sell.

Since Grandpa quit milking, science has gotten more involved in the farming industry and increased productivity. It has become common for farming corporations to inject their cows with hormones to make their muscles grow faster and leaner or to increase their milk production. The same goes for chickens, which are injected with estrogen to make their breasts larger and increase their egg production. Unfortunately those hormones cannot be removed from the animal products by processing or cooking, which means we consume engineered hormones when we eat traditional proteins: meat, milk, cheese, yogurt, and eggs.

Hormones in our animal products aren't the only things "Grandpa wouldn't recognize" along the perimeter of the grocery store. All that beautiful produce has similarly gotten attention from science. Again to increase productivity for a growing population, many varieties have been genetically engineered to reduce disease, and all have been grown among pesticides. No matter how hard you try, you can't wash off chemicals. It's like your favorite moisturizer: you spray it on the skin, but the flesh absorbs it. And what do pesticides and other chemicals act like inside our bodies? Hormones.[2]

To eat fruits and vegetables like those my grandparents ate, we must buy organic produce. The cheapest solution David and I found to this problem was joining a CSA (community-supported agriculture). Every week between June and December, a farmer in our area gives me a share of his harvest for the oh-so-low price of a thousand dollars per year. This requires not only a financial but a time commitment. Every Monday evening during those months is devoted to washing and "putting up" vegetables the way my grandmother used to do on Grandpa's farm. I've become the proud owner of a pressure cooker and a canner—two appliances my mother joyously unburdened herself of two decades ago. We were given an old Blue Bunny deep freezer to keep all our processed-by-me vegetables (the half cow lives there too), and we've learned to eat seasonally. Every summer day my lunch includes a ripe tomato topped with fresh basil slivers, salt, and pepper. Every Thanksgiving I make butternut-squash-something-or-other for David's twenty-six-member family, and every spring we eat salads until we think we'll explode. Seasonal eating is an adjustment, but it is healthier and cheaper in the end.

Seasonal eating is an adjustment, but it is healthier and cheaper in the end.

Just as the milking machine changed Grandpa's life, preprocessed foods changed Grandma's. She also may have gently scolded me for abandoning the center aisles of the grocery store because canned green beans, Bunny bread, and Jell-O freed her from the kitchen. It probably never occurred to her to read the labels on packaging, but if she did, she'd find unpronounceable chemical preservatives and refined sugar. Lots of sugar.[3]

I'm a bit embarrassed to admit that I watch the show *Supernatural*. My bestie got David and me hooked on it. Season seven of the show wasn't stellar, but it managed to reinforce the food changes I was making. The basic premise is that some monsters bought a high-fructose corn syrup company and began pumping the sugar into all food products in America. The sugar fattened the consumers and made them sluggish—so they would be easy for the monsters to catch and tasty for them to eat. The heroes of the show, Sam and Dean, recognize the lethargy of their fellow customers while they are shopping in a convenience store. They begin reading labels:

Sam: It's the corn syrup. Everything in this store is laced with it.

Dean (crestfallen)**:** Everything? [*now frustrated*] Hey, man, I'm gonna go into toxic shock, okay? I need my road food.

Sam: Yeah, that's what [the monster] is banking on.

Dean (holding up a pie)**:** Hey, hey, this one says "natural." That means it's safe, right?

Sam: I hate to break it to you, but corn syrup *is* natural. Technically.

Dean: Well, then, what are we supposed to eat? (Sam holds up a basket with bananas inside.)[4]

Yes, corn syrup is natural, but it is highly processed. The more foods are processed, the harder it is for our bodies to recognize them and utilize the nutrients. This is where we have to evaluate our priorities: are we willing to give up time and money to feed ourselves the best food possible? Most of us would buy organic produce to blend into baby food, but will we cook it for ourselves instead of stopping at a fast-food restaurant on our way home from the grocery store? To feel our best, we need to consume foods made entirely of natural ingredients that our bodies recognize as food.

If I needed more reinforcement that real food is necessary, it came in the fall of 2013 (as I was writing this book). David and I spent huge blocks of time living in hotels that provided "free" breakfasts. Upon first glance the spread was impressive: pastries, bagels, jams and jellies, scrambled eggs, sausage, biscuits, pancakes, yogurt, juice, and coffee. Upon closer inspection, the bread products were all made of highly processed flour and sugar, the eggs were "imitation," the sausage had more filler than actual meat, the yogurt was artificially flavored, and the juice was "from concentrate." I lamented to David, "There's no actual *food* here!" After three months of this breakfast, I'd gained ten pounds, had persistent gastrointestinal pain, was losing gallbladder function, and was—for the first time in my life—a coffee addict.

Avery's Story

Growing up as a young lady in the South, it is almost predetermined that upon completing college, the next step is to get married and have children. While that is a wonderful thought, it does not happen for everyone. Some women choose different career paths, side-stepping wedding plans and motherhood altogether. Others choose to get married, but they do not seem interested in having children. In many ways I wanted the traditional plan, thinking family life would just fall into place. Most good things require hard work, but having children seemed like more of a gift that I expected to receive at the appropriate time.

Early in my high school years, I experienced complications with my cycle. The consensus from different doctors was that I should take birth control pills to regulate my periods, and eventually my body would sort itself out.

A few years later, in my mid-twenties, I continued to have pain each month without much relief. Finally a doctor proposed I have laparoscopic surgery, which revealed endometriosis. I was both devastated and relieved. For the first time the possibility of not having children entered my mind. This disease did not have a cure, and little progress had been made in the field of medicine to discover new treatment methods. Thus I was put on birth control again.

A couple of years later, I married an amazing guy named Daniel. Our lives fit comfortably like two peas in a pod. At first we were enjoying life together and were not focused on having children. Although it was very much in the back of my mind, I felt we had time.

After three or four years went by, I began to wonder why I had not gotten pregnant yet. We were not really trying to have a baby, but we were not doing anything to prevent a pregnancy either. When I turned thirty I started to wonder, *Have I missed my moment of opportunity?* Most of my friends had gotten pregnant by now, and I was starting to get anxious. All along I knew God had a plan, but sometimes it is so hard to trust that He knows best. I wanted my faith to be stirred, to believe that He really could do anything. The scary question was, am I even supposed to be a mom?

I decided I needed to make some changes. I have always struggled with my weight, but in my twenties it became a bigger issue in my life. I tried so many diets, but none really worked that well. After several failed attempts at trendy diets and even taking diet

I knew God had a plan, but sometimes it is so hard to trust that He knows best.

pills, I began researching what I could do to get healthy. I realized the up-and-down roller coaster of dieting was not a solution. The habits of unhealthy eating would not be broken easily, and I wanted to do something that I could sustain for years to come.

Daniel was very encouraging and helpful in this process, and the adjustments had to be gradual in order to become a part of our routine. I started introducing healthy options. I researched blogs on eating healthy, clean eating, and ways to transition to a more organic lifestyle. My goal was not to become a health nut, just to become healthier. I did not lose a considerable amount right away, but the changes we were making were actually working. Except for occasionally eating out, we removed most of the preservatives and

My goal was not to become a health nut, just to become healthier.

artificial foods from our diets. I began cooking with more whole foods and produce, shopping at farmer's markets, and looking for recipes that included more foods that our bodies need. By paying closer attention to my body, I also learned what foods are a challenge for my body to process. By avoiding these foods most of the time, I feel considerably better.

After a little research about natural ways to regulate hormones, I began taking evening primrose oil supplements. I did not always take it as directed; I would take it a few times a week and sometimes miss a week altogether. After about a year I noticed my cycle was gradually regulating. This was extremely odd for me because I had always experienced irregular cycles, sometimes going months in between my periods.

The regular cycles continued for about a year, and out of the blue, I became pregnant. Daniel and I were thrilled. We were also amazed that five years into our marriage, we were finally going to have a baby. Between the sixth and seventh week, I had an ultrasound to confirm the baby was healthy. We saw our baby's little heart beating away. The next few weeks were filled with excitement and anticipation.

Around the fourteenth week, we went to the doctor for a checkup. I had begun to have some complications. I was scared but trying to remain hopeful. The doctor scheduled an ultrasound right away, and immediately my fears were realized. I had miscarried. I remember all I could do for days, and even months, was cry. The thought of losing something so precious, so beautiful, is a kind of pain I can't explain. Sometimes I wondered if I would ever get beyond that season, ever experience the joys of another.

I still don't know the answers to those questions, but I can honestly say that I am still hopeful. As I get closer and closer to thirty-five, I constantly wonder, *Will I experience the blessing of being a mother someday?* It is frustrating at times, but I am inspired by other women in my life who have walked a similar road. Some have eventually been able to conceive while others remained barren, but they have all brought me much encouragement either way.

"Your skin is your biggest organ . . ."

David's and my quest for natural hormone balance had a two-pronged approach. First was purifying what we put *in* our bodies; second was purifying what we put *on* our bodies. Our fertility doctor told me that artificial hormones are all around us. They can be found in the air-freshened oxygen we breathe, the petroleum-based carpets and engineered-hardwood floors we walk on, the paraben-preserved cosmetics we use, and the stain-resistant clothing we wear. Dr. Walter J. Crinnon explained in the introduction to his study on parabens and phthalates:

> Some environmental toxins like DDT and other chlorinated compounds accumulate in the body because of their fat-soluble nature. Other compounds do not stay long in the body, but still cause toxic effects during the time they are present. For serious health problems to arise, exposure to these rapidly-clearing compounds must occur on a daily basis. Two such classes of compounds are the phthalate plasticizers and parabens, both of which are used in many personal care products, some medications, and even foods and food preservation. The phthalates are

commonly found in foods and household dust. Even though they have relatively short half-lives in humans, phthalates have been associated with a number of serious health problems, including infertility, testicular dysgenesis, obesity, asthma, and allergies, as well as leiomyomas and breast cancer. Parabens, which can be dermally absorbed, are present in many cosmetic products, including antiperspirants. Their estrogenicity and tissue presence are a cause for concern regarding breast cancer. Fortunately, these compounds are relatively easy to avoid and such steps can result in dramatic reductions of urinary levels of these compounds.[5]

So, guess what: label reading doesn't stop when you leave the grocery store.

Even if you only use vinegar and lemons to clean your kitchen, your home is still permeated with chemicals. Name a building material—any building material—drywall, flame-retardant insulation, plastic plumbing, caulking. They all contain toxic chemicals, but who would want to live in a house without them? As I see it, the only way to have the perfect environment for conception is to row your own wooden boat to a deserted island, where you cut down your own trees to build your hut and decorate your living room with coconut shells and palm fronds. There you can eat only wild-grown fruit and wild-caught fish while drinking only water from a natural stream. It's a wonder children are conceived anywhere on earth besides the set of *Survivor*.

It is impractical if not impossible to remove all contaminants from our lives. What we can do is control what we put in and on our bodies.

You may have noticed commercials for prescription "patches" on television. I used to associate patches with nicotine addiction or sorority sisters trying to lose a few pounds, but prescription medications of all kinds are now manufactured as patches. I've used a lidocaine patch for back pain, and I know people who have used estrogen patches for HRT and testosterone patches for Low T. If our skin didn't provide a quick delivery system from the epidermis to the bloodstream, pharmaceutical companies would have stuck with pills and shots for all our drug needs.

Unfortunately our skin is indiscriminate: it will absorb whatever it comes in contact with, including your favorite paraben-preserved moisturizer.

Take your food-label skills to the cosmetics department, and purchase products with simple ingredients. Look for words that have *phthalate* or *paraben* in them, and put those boxes back on the shelf. Beware that healthy products will not have preservatives in them, so fight the urge to buy in bulk, no matter how good the sale is! While I typically live by the mantra "Waste not, want not," I admit that I did clean out all paraben-containing cosmetics under my bathroom sink when I got home from the aforementioned doctor's appointment. I also started eliminating plastic food-storage containers. I decided those were effective changes I could make immediately without losing too much money.

When you make your cosmetic and storage purchases, go back to the idea that you don't want to own anything your grandmother wouldn't recognize. This means natural ingredients and a lot of heavy glass items. An invaluable resource for me is GoodGuide. There's a website and a phone app that quickly rate how healthy an item is. You'll learn some surprising

Look for words that have *phthalate* or *paraben* in them, and put those boxes back on the shelf.

things from the GoodGuide; for example, plain-old Shout laundry pre-treater is 100 percent healthy.[6] No need to spend extra money on those "green" brands that tend to be more expensive and often don't work as well. Then you can abandon all your technology and save money by hitting garage sales. As our grandmothers are selling their old glass jars, we can snatch them up! The glass jars never deteriorate, and you can purchase only the pop tops when those wear out from multiple canning sessions.

For a list of books and websites that helped me make healthy lifestyle changes, see the Suggested Resources section beginning on page 132.

As you make these changes, your body will thank you. You will even get to a point when your pocketbook will thank you. Buying whole cows, hunting wild animals, canning seasonal vegetables, and using glass containers for decade after decade saves money over time. The initial start-up cost of switching to a healthier lifestyle is daunting, so don't try to do it overnight. Every little change you make—even if it is trading one fast-food meal for one homemade seasonal meal—is beneficial. What isn't beneficial is making yourself a nervous wreck in an attempt to be "perfect."

"Stop stressing . . ."

Did you catch the second part of what our doctor told us? "Do your best never to shop at a grocery store. *But don't get obsessed about it.*" Why? Because stress affects your hormones, of course! When humans feel any kind of pressure, from trying to meet a work deadline to timing intercourse with ovulation, our bodies have a primordial fight-or-flight response. Our brains begin to shut off nonessential functions, such as ovulation, as they go into survival mode, and we release *cortisol*, a hormone that suppresses the immune system (as hydrocortisone suppresses allergic reactions) and increases blood sugar. If your body is concerned with staying alive, then it isn't going to be able to create and support a second life. We must learn to manage our stress.

"Get moving—but don't do too much!"

What is the number-one most-effective way to manage stress? Exercise! I personally hate exercise. I don't like to be sweaty, and I don't like to shower every day. Hot showers and hard water dry out my skin, and it takes much too long to straighten my mane of red hair. I know I am not alone in this. At the least I inherited the attitude from my mother!

I have learned to fool myself into getting exercise. I do activities that burn calories but that don't feel like work. I've practiced yoga for the last five years or so. Yoga is great for stress management and loosening my back muscles after a day at the computer desk. My favorite part is at the end of the hour, when Miss Evelyn says to us, "You have nothing else to do right now but relax." Imagine Japanese bells dinging in the background and a cool breeze from the ceiling fans, and you might understand my addiction.

I've always been an avid swimmer—in spite of the skin-drying chlorinated water—and a "good walker." I could have easily kept up with the quintessential "good walkers," the Misses Musgrove, as they crossed fields to visit their friends in *Persuasion*.[7] I got this from my mother, too, because as I kid I trailed behind her everywhere she went. I may be short, but I use every inch of my leg length.

Since moving out west, I've translated my "good walking" into hiking. When we go into the mountains, David and I get to explore nature and

Men must check with their doctors to find out exactly how much exercise is right for them.

burn calories together. Exercise is just as important to male fertility as it is to female fertility. Studies show that exercising for one hour, four days per week improves sperm quality. However, vigorous activities, such as cycling or marathon-running, decrease sperm quality. Men must check with their doctors to find out exactly how much exercise is right for them.

Similarly, women need to talk with their doctors about exercise. Daily exercise to manage stress is a good idea regardless of your weight, but women who are not overweight should avoid high-intensity workouts because they can affect the menstrual cycle. If you are overweight, then the best thing you can do for your body is lose that weight. Hormones and chemicals are stored in fat, so as long as you have excess fat, your body will be fighting with itself for balance. The benefits of a healthy body weight far outweigh the potential negatives of too much exercise.[8]

"*Moderation is almost always best* . . ."

It takes a lot of work to remove chemicals and hormones from your world, but it doesn't need to be overwhelming or all-consuming. Make changes one at a time, and do not allow the lifestyle change to become your life. There will be times when you go out to eat at a nonorganic restaurant or are invited into friends' homes for dinner. They probably won't have the same dietary concerns that you do, but don't exalt your dietary preferences over your relationship. Remember what Jesus said to the seventy disciples as He sent them into the mission field: "Stay where you're welcomed. *Become part of the family,* eating and drinking whatever they give you" (Luke 10:7). Paul expounded this idea when he was asked by some Jewish Christians if they should break kosher to dine with non-Jewish Christians:

> We should stop looking out for our own interests and instead focus on the people living and breathing around us. Feel free to eat any meat sold in the market without your conscience raising questions about scruples because "the earth and all that's upon it belong to the Lord." So if some unbelievers invite you to dinner and you want to go, feel free to eat whatever they offer you without raising questions about conscience. . . . So *you ask,* "Why should I give up my freedom to accommodate the scruples of another?" or, "If I am eating with gratitude to God, why am I insulted for eating food that I have properly given thanks for?" *These are good questions.*
>
> Whatever you do—whether you eat or drink *or not*—do it all to the glory of God! Do not offend Jews or Greeks or any part of the church of God *for that matter. Consider my example:* I strive to please all people in all my actions and words. (1 Cor. 10:24–33)

People are more important to God than rules. Your relationships should be more important to you than a few lifestyle changes. Eating one nonorganic piece of chicken and complimenting its chef won't kill you, but it may enliven your relationship with a new friend. More practically—and on a completely selfish note—it is possible you would want that friend to bring you a benevolence meal when you get home from the hospital. Nonorganic chicken baked for you by someone else beats organic chicken that stays raw in the refrigerator any day!

Questions

1. What do you put in or on your body that maybe you shouldn't?

2. How do you manage stress? Is it an effective strategy?

3. What are your favorite ways to get exercise? Are you doing too little? Too much?

4. Have you become obsessed with conceiving? How has it impacted your relationships, and what do behaviors do you need to change?

CHAPTER SIX

"Maybe You Waited Too Long"

Reaching a Career Goal Before Starting a Family

Women growing up over the last thirty years have consistently received mixed messages about who they should aspire to be when they grow up. We start out loving our Disney princesses, pretending to be Snow White waiting in the forest for Prince Charming's kiss, or Sleeping Beauty waiting in a tower for Prince Philip's kiss, or the Little Mermaid waiting on the boat for Prince Eric's kiss. Or Cinderella waiting for her lost shoe.

In middle school we realize that marrying a prince is not only unlikely but also a waste of our personal talents. We learn world history, and our textbooks emphasize the (sometimes overblown) roles women have had in the world's development. We are told we can do anything we want to do; we are told not to waste the opportunities created for us by suffragettes, Rosie the Riveter, and bra burners. If you are part of Generation X or the Millennials, this message was reinforced as you personally witnessed a lot of firsts for American women:

- 1981: Sandra Day O'Connor was the first woman appointed to the Supreme Court.

- 1983: Sally Ride was the first woman in space.

- 1984: Geraldine Ferraro was the first woman to run for vice president on a major party ticket.

- 1993: Janet Reno was the first woman appointed U.S. attorney general.

- 1997: Madeline Albright was the first woman appointed secretary of state.

- 1999: Nancy Ruth Mace was the first female cadet to graduate from the Citadel.

- 2007: Drew Gilpin Faust was the first woman selected president of Harvard University.

- 2010: Kathryn Bigelow was the first woman to win Best Director at the Academy Awards.

- 2012: Ginni Rometty was the first woman appointed CEO of IBM.

In my lifetime, women have made strides in the fields of government, science, art, education, and business; and yes, they have built upon foundations dug by their feminist ancestors. I am thankful for all they've accomplished and realize I probably wouldn't have been offered a Harvard education without them. I certainly wouldn't be writing a book about infertility.

The opportunities still available in America are truly inspiring to girls everywhere who dream of being the first female president of the United States. But is there an unintended consequence? Girls learn quickly that the correct answer to "What do you want to be when you grow up?" is not "A wife and mother." It is "A lawyer," "A doctor," or "A governor." As more of us have achieved high degrees and attained higher-paying jobs than ever before, the opportunity to be a mother and have a "fairy-tale ending" has been almost magically transformed into a challenge.

"What glass ceiling?"

Women had a banner year in 2011: we now hold more advanced degrees than men do.[1] We surpassed them in undergraduate degrees a long time ago, but the fact that universities are now graduating more female doctors and lawyers than their male counterparts indicates a coming permanent shift in the male–female balance of power in the professional world and in the home. But we aren't there quite yet.

As more and more of us trade in our remaining glass slipper for better traction on the climb toward the glass ceiling over our chosen careers, we still have to work harder than men. According to the U.S. Department of Labor:

- Between 1979 and 2011, women's-to-men's earnings ratios rose for most age groups. Among 25- to 34-year-olds, for example, the ratio grew from 68 percent in 1979 to 92 percent in 2011.

- Among the age groupings of those 35 years and older, women had earnings that ranged from 75 percent to 81 percent of those of their male counterparts.

- Women are more likely than men to work in professional and related occupations. Within this occupational category, though, the proportion of women employed in the higher paying job groups is much smaller than the proportion of men employed in them.

- Of the 44.5 million women working full time in wage and salary jobs in 2011, a little more than one-third were mothers of children under age 18.[2]

The bottom line: women still make less than their male counterparts, although the number of women in the workforce is increasing and we are more likely than men to join white-collar careers. If we are better educated, why are we behind in earnings? Is it because most women still split their time and attention between work and home? When it comes to building a family, we are at an anatomical disadvantage compared to our husbands that can't be overcome without an adjustment of priorities or a boatload of money.

Let's assume you're a lawyer, fresh out of your clerkship and finally starting work at a law firm. You are twenty-six years old. You want to

We are at an anatomical disadvantage compared to our husbands that can't be overcome without an adjustment of priorities or a boatload of money.

climb that corporate ladder you just dropped $180,000 in student loans to mount, and you know it will take long, late hours to do it. You decide to push off having children until you've moved up because, you reason, it will be easier to take maternity leave just after receiving a promotion instead of before one is awarded to you. By the time that promotion comes, you are thirty. This job requires even longer hours and more responsibility, and you couldn't have children right now even if you wanted to: you haven't had a period in almost a year because of the stress. At your insurance-mandated annual gynecology appointment, that fact comes up. Your doctor recommends that you have some lab work done to identify the problem, and the next thing you know, you're being told it's now-or-never time for starting a family while you're simultaneously trying to answer e-mails on your smartphone.

If you were a man, you might have had a child at any point in that scenario because most fathers take less than two weeks of paternity leave.[3] Most women take two to three months of maternity leave, and that's after already missing a lot of work for doctors' appointments and morning sickness during the pregnancy. That's a shame, but that's anatomy! The babies must grow inside of mothers instead of fathers, and there is nothing we can do about it.

✳ Jess's Story ✳

College was completed, grad school was done, and the guy I dated all those years didn't turn out to be "the one." That was okay; I was a twentysomething professional enjoying a challenging job as a children's librarian with the Los Angeles Public Library. Sure I spent three hours in my car each day commuting between an apartment I could barely afford with two roommates and my workplace in downtown LA, but I told myself I was enjoying being single and free even if it wasn't what I had in mind when I went off to college. And yet something was still missing.

Almost on a whim one day I started looking for jobs in my field that would take me anywhere to get me out of the life I was no longer able to pretend I wanted. I widened my search to include private-sector positions and moved in 2002 to Maryland, where I started working for a book distributor. For several more years I was able to pretend that my life was complete, and yet there was still this thought that I wasn't where I needed to be.

Wandering through the stacks of the Baltimore Public Library one day, I started browsing the 200s and ran across a book by Dr. Henry Cloud entitled, *How to Get a Date Worth Keeping: Be Dating in Six Months or Your Money Back*. I recognized his name from the popular book *Boundaries* that he had coauthored with Dr. John Townsend, so I took it home. He told the story of a woman who insisted God would bring a husband to her doorstep without any help from her. He told her, "If you don't want to marry the FedEx man or a Jehovah's Witness, you had better go outside!"[4] For me, "going outside" meant someplace other than house, car, work, or church. If I wanted to have a relationship, it was time to meet new people.

In April 2007 I joined a science-fiction book club, intending to meet someone with whom I'd been swapping e-mails. I found out just before the meeting that he wouldn't be attending that night, but I decided to go anyway.

We were reading Naomi Novik's *His Majesty's Dragon*. I enjoyed the book and the people who were there. So I decided to go again the next month. I liked meeting the guy I'd been e-mailing; however, there was someone else who caught my eye, this cocky guy named Aidan. When he showed up at the May meeting, I didn't trust him and his balancing-on-two-legs-of-his-chair confidence. I was convinced he would play me and break my heart. However, we had a lot friends in common, so we were soon hanging out whether I wanted to spend time with him or not. He wasn't quite so put off

It's possible to balance motherhood and career.

by me; by October I had turned down his invitations to two weddings. On his third attempt, he asked me to dinner at his house. His being a fantastic cook, it was not our last meal together. He proposed 365 days later, and we married May 2009.

We started trying to have children May 2010. When nothing had happened by December, I went to my gynecologist, who put me on prenatal vitamins. I was pregnant by March 2011, but by the April 13 checkup, I didn't feel pregnant anymore. The ultrasound technician and the doctor were both unable to find the heartbeat. As I shared the sad news with friends and family, love manifested around Aidan and me. Tragically, two of my friends had miscarriages the same month I did, so we supported each other, and their husbands helped Aidan walk through his grief. His father had died April 2010, just short of our one-year anniversary, so the help of our friends was a double blessing.

The following December we started trying again, and February 2012 I turned forty and discovered I was pregnant. In April I again lost the baby naturally, so my gynecologist referred us to a local fertility clinic. It was a miserable experience, punctuated by the doctor's comment, "In an ideal world, I'd reverse your age with your husband's." They had no practical solutions for us. Everyone there made me feel old—as if babies made in me weren't meant to live. Thirty-five-year-old Aidan was fine. It was all my body, all my fault.

I made my peace with God that we wouldn't have kids. I had a good career, an aging body, and no local family support. I was okay, but Aidan wasn't ready to not be a dad. He reminded me that so often in his life, "the third time's the charm," which was true (such as when I finally agreed to a date). When a friend recommended a reproductive endocrinologist whom she highly respected, Aidan and I agreed to try again and made an appointment for June 2012. While filling out the extensive paperwork for the appointment, I realized I was pregnant. The doctor's office confirmed it, and he treated me as he would any high-risk pregnancy. Our sweet baby Liam was born February 12, 2013. I'll be fifty-nine when he graduates high school.

I am learning that it's possible to balance motherhood and career. In the private sector, I can't take even one year off and come back to the same position. Technology changes too fast, and office politics never go on maternity leave. But I don't have to be a stay-at-home mom or a part-time librarian because we have found a family to care for Liam during the week as if he were their own. He never lacks for attention or love, and I don't have to stop my career in its tracks.

"You can have it all, but it won't be easy . . ."

What happens as this need to satisfy social milieus and our personal dreams pushes marriage and pregnancy into our thirties? into our forties? Quite simply, it is going to be harder to conceive, carry, and deliver a healthy child. The number of women facing this reality increases every year. The birth rate among American women in their forties has increased by more than 70 percent since 1990, and the birth rate among women between thirty-five and thirty-nine has increased more than 50 percent.[5] Those increases reflect how many women are giving birth—not how many are trying to get pregnant. There is an obvious shift in the demographic of aspiring mothers.

We broached the topic of fertility challenges in older women in chapter 1. To review:

- As a woman's age increases, the time it takes her to get pregnant also increases.

- Women under the age of thirty have a 71 percent chance of conceiving; women over the age of thirty-six have a 41 percent chance.

- For every five years of age, a woman's body is 10 percent more likely to spontaneously abort a pregnancy due to chromosomal abnormalities.[6]

This isn't ageism; it's fact. The longer you wait to get pregnant, the harder it will be. Our bodies were designed to have children when we were in our late teens and twenties. Just ask those Disney princesses. Snow White, Aurora, and Ariel were fourteen, sixteen, and sixteen, respectively, when they married their princes and presumably started producing heirs. By the pre-Industrial Revolution timetable, we're all dusty old maids (like poor nineteen-year-old Cinderella) before we graduate from high school. Forget about higher education.

As women have thrived in the workforce, science has done a pretty good job of keeping up with us. In their day, our Disney princesses might have been beheaded and replaced (à la Anne Boleyn and company) if they couldn't produce heirs. Two to three millennia before them, everyone's favorite matriarch, Rachel, only had two options to overcome her barrenness: old-fashioned surrogacy, where you beg your husband to sleep with the nanny (Gen. 30:3); or natural fertility drugs, which you get by pimping out said husband to your sister (Gen. 30:14–16). Today we have medical options that don't run the risk of severing our marriage covenants or our necks. The two most common versions of assisted reproductive therapy (ART) are intrauterine insemination (IUI) and in vitro fertilization (IVF).

IUI

By far the oldest form of ART, intrauterine insemination, was first used in animals and humans in the eighteenth century. Sperm are taken from a male donor and injected into the female uterus with a catheter. Awaiting my first round of IUI, I admit the image of the Triple Crown–winning

> ### Today we have medical options that don't run the risk of severing our marriage covenants or our necks.

horse Secretariat and his 653 foals ran through my mind, as did a few requisite turkey-baster jokes.

As technology has advanced, the procedure has become more complex and more accurate. Fertility clinics realize we aren't beasts. They chart a woman's cycle, sometimes giving her fertility drugs and/or injectable hormones to increase the number of mature follicles her ovaries produce during one cycle. When it has been determined via urine test, blood test, or ultrasound that she is ovulating, the man gives a sperm sample. Within one hour, that deposit is "washed" so that the best sperm are removed from the seminal fluid and concentrated. A doctor then injects the sperm into the uterus with a plastic medical catheter, and the woman lies on her back for about ten minutes. Two weeks later she'll take a pregnancy test.

Fertility clinics estimate that 60 percent of qualified couples will conceive via IUI within six cycles of treatment.

This form of assisted reproductive therapy is comparatively inexpensive, costing about one thousand dollars per session for the steps described. It is noninvasive, has few if any side effects, and takes fewer than ninety minutes from sample to injection. Every cycle of IUI has a success rate of approximately 12 percent, and fertility clinics estimate that 60 percent of qualified couples will conceive via IUI within six cycles of treatment. Those aren't bad odds—though not nearly as good as Secretariat's 1-to-10 odds at his last Triple Crown race.

IVF

As described in chapter 2, in vitro fertilization didn't appear until the late 1970s. Compared to IUI, it is in its infancy. Elizabeth Comeau, the first American conceived via IVF, was born in 1981. Her doctors and her parents had to jump through legal and ethical hoops before the procedure could be performed, and although IVF is almost common today, some ethical issues remain.

The IVF procedure begins just before ovulation, when a woman's follicles are about to release eggs. As with IUI, she may have been advised by her doctor to take fertility drugs and/or use injectable hormones to develop an above-average number of follicles in one cycle. The woman then must go under general anesthesia so the doctor can perform an ultrasound-guided aspiration, injecting a hollow tube into each mature follicle and sucking out the egg. Meanwhile, the man makes a sperm deposit. Technicians will fertilize the eggs in a laboratory and wait as long as a week to see if the fertilized eggs grow into embryos. The successful embryos are then implanted in the uterus with a catheter, the woman stays on her back for one to six hours (depending on the doctor's orders), and two weeks later she takes a pregnancy test.

IVF is expensive and invasive. The national average for one cycle of IVF using fresh eggs and fresh sperm (not from donors) is $8,158.[7] Part of the cost is hospital fees; IVF often requires hospital admittance, anesthesia, and postoperative pain medication following egg retrieval. Every cycle has an average success rate of approximately 22 percent. As with pregnancy in general, the younger you are, the higher your success rate. Women under age thirty-five have a 35 percent success rate, while women over forty have an 11 percent success rate.

All forms of ART require you to decide at the outset if you believe God has given humanity fertility treatments so we can have children, or if you believe humans are "playing God" by creating life. My mother faced this conundrum before taking Clomid to have me, and David and I faced it as we researched ART. IVF also requires you to consider, when does life begin? If your answer is "At conception," then you will need to design your IVF treatment around the number of embryos the lab creates.

Because of IVF's high cost, doctors like to extract as many eggs as possible from the woman so they can create as many embryos as possible. It is possible that a couple could have as many as ten embryos from one round of laboratory fertilization. That is when decisions must be made.

1. How many embryos will you have implanted at once?

2. If you have too many embryos implant successfully, will you allow "selective reduction" to preserve the lives of the saved babies and yourself?

3. How long will you leave your embryos frozen between pregnancies?

4. What will you do with the "extra" embryos when you are finished having children?

The last question is the hardest. Your options are disposal, donation to an infertile couple, or donation to medical research. None of these answers is ideal.[8] Only donation to an infertile couple preserves the life of the embryo; but there is no guarantee that an embryo will ever be adopted, and parents are left wondering, *Do I have more children?* and, *Who is raising my child?* To avoid these questions altogether, you can tell your laboratory to attempt only a specified number of embryos. This lowers your chance of IVF success and raises the potential cost of conception, but it may be the ethical solution that works for you.

"You're a smart girl. You should have made a better plan . . ."

Once doctors diagnose you as infertile, an invisible clock starts in your head. If you are over thirty, then it's moving a little faster than that of the younger women around you. There is so much to learn about reproductive physiology, treatment options, financial responsibilities, and even ethical conundrums. We all do the best we can with the information we have, but sometimes hurried decisions may not have received the vetting they deserved.

Inevitably you will face a moment when you question every decision you ever made—from accepting the international fellowship that delayed your marriage by two years to drinking the second glass of red wine last night that made you woozy. People around you will fill your head with "woulda, shoulda, coulda," thinking they are helping you reason but only making you more miserable. Don't become a victim of guilt. Don't let others force it on you, and don't take it upon yourself.

The apostles Mark and Luke both tell the story of a woman who had been bleeding for twelve years. They don't name her, but a fourth-century extrabiblical text called the *Acts of Pilate* identifies her as "Bernice." She is the only character in the New Testament who presents with what is obviously a menstrual disorder. As you read Mark's account, picture this woman. Based on the length of her illness, she was probably in her thirties and unmarried. Her disease had kept her from enjoying Jerusalem's society because the blood flow made her unclean. And she'd been disappointed by doctor after doctor who had taken her money and given her nothing but dashed hopes and more grief.

In the crowd pressing around Jesus, there was a woman who had suffered continuous bleeding for 12 years, *bleeding that made her ritually unclean and an outcast according to the purity laws.* She had suffered greatly; and although she spent all her money on her medical care, she had only gotten worse. She had heard of this *Miracle-Man,* Jesus, so she snuck up behind Him in the crowd and reached out her hand to touch His cloak.

Woman *(to herself):* Even if all I touch are His clothes, I know I will be healed.

As soon as her fingers brushed His cloak, the bleeding stopped. She could feel that she was whole again.

Lots of people were pressed against Jesus at that moment, but He immediately felt her touch; He felt healing power flow out of Him.

He stopped. Everyone stopped. He looked around.

Jesus: Who just touched My robe?

His disciples broke the uneasy silence.

Disciples: Jesus, the crowd is so thick that everyone is touching You. Why do You ask, "Who touched Me?"

But Jesus waited. His gaze swept across the crowd to see who had done it. At last, the woman—knowing He was talking about her—pushed forward and dropped to her knees.

She was shaking with fear *and amazement.*

Woman: *I touched You.*

Then she told Him the reason why. *Jesus listened to her story.*

Jesus: Daughter, you are well because you *dared* to believe. Go in peace, and stay well. (Mark 5:24–34)

Bernice had done the best she could for herself with the tools she had. Her whole life had become about her disease: she was constantly managing the blood flow (which meant changing clothes, washing herself, and doing laundry multiple times per day), she was in and out of doctors' offices, and she had no social life.

> ## Praise God for what He gives you and for what He takes away. Then you can be free of guilt and may also be a blessing to others.

I assume she made no apologies for the way she had lived her life—not even when she broke every social convention by appearing in public without a male relative, ritually impurifying anyone who came in physical contact with her, and talking to a recognized rabbi. There may have been a lot of instances when she felt guilty in the past twelve years, but when she was directly confronted by Jesus for touching His robe—an action she couldn't possibly know the consequence of—she took responsibility, told Him her story, and received a blessing from Him. Her story has gone on to bless two millennia of readers.

Imitate Bernice. Do the best you can with the information you have. Trust in God, and pray that the Holy Spirit will guide your actions. Praise God for what He gives you and for what He takes away. Then you can be free of guilt and may also be a blessing to others.

Questions

1. How do you perceive stay-at-home moms versus career women? Do you respect one more than the other? Why?

2. Which is more attractive to you: the fairy tale associated with finding the glass slipper or the secular success associated with breaking the glass ceiling? How would either scenario fit into your family planning?

3. If you have a more lucrative career than your husband, would you be willing to let him become a stay-at-home dad while you are the breadwinner? Why or why not?

4. How would you address the ethical issues that come from embryo creation and IVF?

5. During your fertility journey, have you done the best you could with the information you had? Do you suffer guilt resulting from the "woulda, shoulda, coulda" questions?

CHAPTER SEVEN

"At Least You Know You Can Get Pregnant"

Coping with the Loss of Pregnancy

Consider two pregnant women: one immediately posts a picture of the positive pregnancy test on Facebook, and one waits to tell even her parents until after the first trimester. If the first miscarries, she's left with the "embarrassing" task of retracting her announcement. If the second miscarries, she's left with only a prickly doctor and an equally sad and confused husband to comfort her. Who made the better decision? Who is better positioned to heal from the loss of her child?

"We aren't sure what happened . . ."

Western society doesn't talk about miscarriages, so we may not realize just how common they are until one happens to us or to someone close to us. According to the American Pregnancy Association, as many as one in four pregnancies will end in a *spontaneous abortion*, commonly and more gently called a *miscarriage*, before gestation reaches twenty weeks. Up to 50 percent of those are *chemical pregnancies*, which self-terminate within the first eight weeks. Most miscarriages will occur before the fourteenth week of pregnancy.[1]

There are myriad situations that can result in miscarriage. The most common problem in early miscarriages is chromosomal abnormality, meaning the cells themselves are damaged in some way and cannot heal. As a gynecologist told my friend Rebecca, "There was no way to save it. There just wasn't enough information in the cells to make a human." (Thanks, doc.) Other factors in early and late miscarriages may include hormone imbalance, ectopic implantation, infection, maternal age, physical injury, or unhealthy lifestyle choices. If you smoke, stop. If you abuse alcohol or drugs, stop. Otherwise miscarriage is never your fault.

The symptoms of a miscarriage are similar in all cases, regardless of the cause, and may resemble menstruation. The mother will experience lower back and abdominal cramping, and then she will pass blood and tissue. The severity of these symptoms depends on the type of miscarriage that is occurring:

Complete Miscarriage: Your body removes all traces of the pregnancy on its own, and any cramping and bleeding subside naturally.

Incomplete Miscarriage: You must take drugs or have an invasive procedure to remove any remaining embryonic tissue in your uterus. Surgery is necessary to stop the cramping and bleeding, and to prevent infection.

Missed Miscarriage: This type of complete miscarriage happens without your knowledge. There is no cramping or bleeding, and the expelled embryo seemingly "disappears."

Recurrent Miscarriage: This label is assigned when there have been three or more consecutive miscarriages (of any type) within the first trimester of the pregnancies.

In the case of the *ectopic pregnancy*, the embryo has implanted outside of the uterus, often inside the fallopian tubes. Because the female reproductive system is not designed to efficiently remove tissue from anywhere other than the uterus, surgical intervention is necessary. The standard of care for ectopic pregnancies is surgical removal of the embryo, either through laparoscopy or a small abdominal incision. This is done to preserve the woman's life (as ectopic pregnancies can cause hemorrhaging,

> **The symptoms of a miscarriage are similar in all cases, regardless of the cause, and may resemble menstruation.**

infection, and death) and minimize damage to her reproductive system. There is a growing use of *expectant management*, where doctors basically "watch and wait." Implanted in a less-blood-rich environment than the uterus, most embryos simply cannot survive. Up to 49 percent of ectopic pregnancies self-terminate.[2]

There are anecdotal cases where the pregnancy developed, a child was born, and the mother lived. These are incredibly rare. It is tempting to cling to those cases with hope—I know—but it is important that you listen to the advice of your doctor. If you've taken the time to choose someone whom you trust and who shares your value system, as we discussed in chapter 2, then rely on that faith you put in him or her and allow your doctor to use his education, training, and experience to heal you.

"Who knows you were pregnant?"

Until the last generation or so, the topic of pregnancy has been taboo. There were no stretchy T-shirts with cute sayings such as, "Caution: Baby Under Construction" or "There's a Pea in My Pod." In polite company pregnant women wore only tentlike dresses that completely covered their changing bodies. Lucille Ball famously appeared on her television show *I Love Lucy* while pregnant, shocking censors and the viewing public. Why? Because if Lucy was pregnant, then she and Desi must have had sex. And we don't even think about sex. Believe it or not, there was a gentler time in television, when primetime viewing wasn't filled with steamy affairs and underage sex. We got our social educations from our parents instead of ratings-minded networks.

From the tragedies came new life for a woman who had been hopeless and lost.

I made the mistake of going to the movie theater to see *The Help* the weekend after my fourth miscarriage.[3] The whole movie is great, but I got caught up in Celia's subplot. Jessica Chastain (who plays me in the beautiful movie-version of my life that sometimes rolls in my head) abandons her naturally red hair to play the blonde, backwoods-raised Celia, who has married into a wealthy family, is hated by the Southern socialites who disapprove of her marriage, and silently suffers from recurrent miscarriages. In a particularly poignant scene, Minny the maid is the first to learn about the miscarriages when she finds Celia in a pool of blood in the bathroom. Minny helps her clean up, bury the baby in the backyard, and plant a rosebush as the grave marker next to three other rosebushes, which are presumably over her previously miscarried children. The book handles the situation a bit differently. There is no memorial for the child; instead, "the nurse walks around . . . and out the back door carrying a white tin box."[4] The book's portrayal of the incident is more callous but probably more realistic for the setting of 1960s Mississippi.

Celia doesn't talk about her miscarriages with anyone, not even her husband. She is so afraid of how others would react to her losses that she allows her neighbors and even her maid to think her erratic behavior is the result of drinking alcohol. When Celia finally tells her husband Johnny what has been going on, she receives the love and support she needs, not the divorce papers she expected. Minny the maid describes the scene:

> "I told him about the baby," Miss Celia whispers. "All the babies."
>
> "Minny, I would've lost her if it hadn't of been for you," he says, grabbing hold of my hands. "Thank God you were here."
>
> I look over at Miss Celia and she looks dead in the eyes. I already know what that doctor told her. I can see it, that there won't ever be any babies born alive. Mister Johnny squeezes my hands, then he goes to her. He gets down on his kneecaps and lays his head down in her lap. She smoothes his hair over and over.
>
> "Don't leave. Don't ever leave me, Celia," he cries.[5]

Celia needed to share her pain with her husband and those who loved her. As she did, she became more confident, and her quality of life improved at home and within Mississippi society. She also learned who her real friends were and just how much her husband loved her. From the tragedies came new life for a woman who had been hopeless and lost.

Leah's Story

When Paul and I married, I was twenty-two and already well acquainted with irregular cycles. I was studying to be a nurse, so my gynecologist had always chalked it up to "young active stress," but when I only had one period the first year of my marriage, I visited a reproductive endocrinologist. He said my initial labs were so bad that Paul and I were in a "now or never" situation. If I hadn't been sitting in front of him, the doctor would have assumed my labs were those of a menopausal woman: high testosterone, low estrogen, trace progesterone. He prescribed Prometrium and Clomid. On a trip to California, Paul and I debated whether or not to fill the prescription. After visiting Disneyland, we knew: this feels right; it is not something we should postpone.

I guess people don't expect a twenty-three-year-old to use fertility drugs, so the reactions we got ranged. My family was thrilled. They saw this as God providing an opportunity, and they encouraged us to take that opportunity. My husband's family had the opposite response. They said that God's timing is perfect, and they told us to wait five years until we were financially stable. Most people landed in the middle: they observed that there's never a "good time" for a baby.

It took two failed months of Clomid and one successful month of Femara. On April Fool's Day we got our positive pregnancy test. I kept saying, "God, if this is not true, then it's a cruel joke!" But it was true, and our sweet Charlotte "Cherry" Faith was born November 17, 2011.

People keep telling me I should be thankful for my one, but I see she's lonely. She loves playing with her cousins and cries whenever we have to leave. Since Cherry was born—as soon as three weeks after I left the hospital—we haven't used contraception because we want her to have a sibling. In May 2012 I found out I was pregnant. At my second ultrasound, the doctor confirmed that I had an empty yolk sac. He said, "There's been no growth in the last week, and it should have doubled in size. I'll send you home with Cytotec to make you flush it out." I was holding Cherry as the doctor was talking. All I could do was stare at a picture of the uterus on his wall. He walked out of the room and I just sat there for five minutes, bawling. Paul was sitting next to me, unsure of what to say or do next, and our seven-month-old was jumping in my lap and completely unaware of what had just happened.

I was scheduled to work that night. The doctor told me I could take the med now or wait a few days—it didn't matter. There was no way I could postpone it. That night I called into work sick, and the charge nurse gave me a hard time. I was nasty to her, started sobbing, and slammed the phone down. In the meantime Paul got home from the pharmacy and grocery store. I immediately took the pill, since I was told it would take about twelve hours to start working. My sweet husband rented a movie for us to watch, one I had been wanting to see for a few months. I ate an entire pint of Ben & Jerry's Chunky Monkey ice cream. He had been so thoughtful, but I couldn't wait to go to bed so he would sleep and I could cry without an audience. I needed my moment to be angry at God. I wanted to ask Him why this had happened. At 2:00 a.m. I woke out of a dead sleep with pain worse than labor. I ran to the bathroom and vomited. I turned to sit on the toilet and sneezed; a perfectly round sack with a string attached to it fell out of me and into the water.

Almost a month after the miscarriage, a friend congratulated me on my pregnancy. She was genuinely excited, but I had to awkwardly explain, "We lost it. A month ago." She didn't know what to say, nor did I, so the conversation just fizzled. But my own family did

How much money and heartache are we willing to invest before we say enough is enough?

know what to say, and it felt like a slap on my hand: "You shouldn't be upset; you have Cherry. Just love her, and everything will be okay. This is part of God's plan." This from a woman who had three perfectly healthy children!

When you have a miscarriage, suddenly all the people in a room with you are pregnant. I was fine with friends' pregnancies until their babies were born. All I have is a date when I know my baby should have been born: February 2, 2013. I'm not someone who can keep having babies only to lose them. I tried to rationalize my pain, telling myself I was glad it happened at eight weeks instead of twenty-eight weeks. But a woman feels so different the moment she finds out she's pregnant; I felt such joy and excitement for our family's future. Then to suddenly have it ripped away—I wouldn't wish that feeling on my worst enemy. The only reason I could pick up and move on was I had a seven-month-old daughter to take care of. My family was right about that. I didn't allow myself to really grieve except for that first week, when our daughter would wake up and cry in the night. I just clung to our sweet baby as we rocked in the rocking chair and I cried with her.

We don't want to focus so much on having another baby that we lose sight of the beautiful little girl we have already been blessed with. We would like to escalate treatment, but it is such a huge expense. How much money and heartache are we willing to invest before we say enough is enough?

"What was your baby's name?"

Science has advanced since Lucy and Celia's time, educating us about our bodies and improving our birth rates. Society no longer sees open discussions of sex and childbearing as taboo. But a mother's ability to process the pain of miscarriage has not evolved one bit.

All women must deal with their miscarriages in uniquely personal ways. I never named my children; I've learned that a lot of women do that. I have a friend who celebrates what would have been her son Jackson's birthday every year. Now that Jackson has three younger sisters, the whole family celebrates by buying what would have been an age-appropriate toy for Jackson and donating it to a community children's home. They also take the opportunity to talk about how God loves all His children—those in heaven and those on earth; those who have mommies and daddies and those who are orphans. She says that as the girls get older, they will use Jackson's birthday to teach the girls that life begins at conception. I can see how that might be a powerful tool. Those girls will understand the sanctity of life (and hopefully the now-countercultural view that sex is only for a husband and wife) better than some of their classmates. Through his family Jackson can make a mark on this world.

We must mourn our miscarriages. We mourn not only the death, but the loss of an unlived life.

I am amazed by how Jackson's family didn't stop with mourning his death but now celebrates the impact he's made on their lives. I could not have this response because it was impossible for me to so openly address the souls that were lost inside my body. I quickly realized that if I dealt with my pain clinically, I could put all the stress of doctors' appointments and lab tests and surgery in a neat "white tin box" and leave my emotions at the hospital. I acted as if those procedures were no different from my childhood tonsillectomy or my more recent ankle-repair surgery. The strategy worked as long as I could stop myself from thinking about my babies as people.

As the miscarriages piled up, I learned to be proactive in my feelings management. The moment I saw a positive pregnancy test, my mind jumped to, *How am I going to lose this one?* There was no joy for the new life growing inside me, only dread of the pain I knew would come in the following weeks. The last time I had a positive pregnancy test, David was out of town on business. I did my usual trek to the doctor for a blood test, and I got home about the same time he did. That night we sat on the couch together, staring at the television and at each other. For hours neither of us said one word. The next day the doctor called to tell me my progesterone was too low to sustain the pregnancy, and that was that.

I soon found myself projecting my fears onto other women. Whenever I see a social-media announcement of a brand-new pregnancy, I worry. I worry that the embryo won't survive and that the mother will soon feel the pain I have felt—but in a public forum. I will never forget the messages a friend of mine received when she "retracted" her pregnancy announcement on Facebook:

Friend One: That sucks! I'm so sorry.

Her Mother-In-Law: Obviously this just wasn't God's plan for you.

Her Sister: You're still the best aunt in the world to my boys!

Work Colleague: Let me know if you need me to cover for you at the office.

Friend Two: You're still so young. Next time things will work out.

Her Father: Don't worry, honey. I didn't want to be a grandfather anyway!

Friend Three: I love you. I'm praying for you.

She received approximately twenty responses before the day was over. Occasionally someone wrote something genuinely supportive, but most people offered her consolation prizes, such as "My kids love you like a mama"; dismissed her pain entirely by saying, "There's always next month"; or managed to make her miscarriage and her pain about themselves: "I didn't want to be a grandfather." Reading those comments, I wished my friend hadn't been so quick to tell the world she was pregnant, but was her experience any worse than my self-induced isolation? No, it was just different.

We must mourn our miscarriages. A miscarriage is the death of a baby, made worse by the fact that no one ever met the little one. We mourn not only the death, but the loss of an unlived life. Without a funeral to push us toward the grieving process, we must find our own ways. I believe our willingness to be open to our pain is a predictor of how quickly we can heal. Don't follow my lead. I avoided my grief for years and compromised my immune system. I was suffering emotionally and physically, so my insightful, beloved, and trusted internist told me to see a talk therapist. After two years of ignoring her ever-so-polite nagging, I went to the psychologist. I learned that health requires a balance between the body, the mind, the emotions, and the spirit. My body was sick because I had been "pushing down" my emotions. The side effect of "pushing" is stress, and stress was making my body sick. I had to break that cycle.

I'm never one to do things halfway (shocking, right?), so I prescribed my own holistic approach to healing that addressed all four parts of me:

1. Body: I recommitted to clean eating, regular workouts, and stress management through yoga and regular sleep. I needed to be healthy for *me*, not just for a baby.

2. Mind: I read and highlighted and internalized the words of every book my therapist recommended about grief and boundaries in my life.

3. Emotions: I learned I was incapable of anger. As a child I had associated anger with hate and misbehavior, which had stunted my emotional development. My doctor helped me understand that anger is a legitimate emotion that is necessary to the healing process.

4. Spirit: I allowed myself to be honest with God about how I felt. I told Him—in a non-hateful and well-behaved way—that I was angry and hurt. My confession made room for Him to heal and to teach me.

These four steps helped me mourn, heal, and move forward with my life. I still feel the pain of a woman who has lost a child—I don't think that will ever go away—but I am now able to see and appreciate how God has used those experiences to bring me closer to Him and (I hope) to help others who are struggling with infertility. Don't spend years pushing down your emotions; face your loss, face your emotions, and turn your face toward God. Only then can He begin to heal you.

For a list of books that helped me better understand my own emotions and how to react properly to them, see the Suggested Resources section beginning on page 132.

"The Bible is silent on this issue . . ."

In chapter 4 Rebecca described how the words of the Bible were hurtful to her after her miscarriages. This is an experience I share. When you've had a miscarriage, it seems the only verse quoted from the pulpit is, "For You shaped me, inside *and out.* / You knitted me together in my mother's womb *long before I took my first breath*" (Ps. 139:13). This psalm of David was written to inspire those who sang it, to remind us that God is with us all the time and everywhere. He was there before we were born; He'll be there after we die. But the grieving mother hears these words and wonders, *Why didn't He bother to knit my baby together?* Because we usually cannot separate our exegesis of scripture from our personal experiences and biases, the thought is understandable—maybe even expected. But feelings of abandonment most certainly are not what God wants us to take away from His scriptures.

Other biblical references to gestation and miscarriage are similarly unhelpful, if not quite so pain-inducing as the psalm. In the laws portion of Exodus, the literal value of unborn life is confirmed. If someone causes another to have a premature stillbirth, then the guilty party is to pay a fine and be killed:

> If *two* men are fighting with each other and *happen to* hit a pregnant woman *during the quarrel* causing her to give birth prematurely (but no other harm is done), then the one who hit her must pay whatever fine the judges determine based upon the amount demanded by the woman's husband.

> But if any further harm comes, then the standard for the punishment is *reciprocal justice*: a life for a life, an eye for an eye, a tooth for a tooth, a hand for a hand, a foot for a foot, a burn for a burn, a wound for a wound, a bruise for a bruise. (Ex. 21:22–25)

On a certain irreverent level, this bit of scripture cracks me up. It is so very specific. It must be based on something that actually happened. I imagine a pregnant woman walking down the dirt road in her ancient city, rubbing her belly, maybe humming to the music she hears in the ancient equivalent of her sound-canceling ear buds. Suddenly—out of nowhere!—a brawl breaks out in the street—unnoticed—*right next to where she is standing*. The fighting men apparently can't see her through the dust they've kicked up, and one of their wild swings accidentally hits her belly. She goes into labor on the spot (while her husband runs to the local judge for a settlement) and presumably gives birth to a healthy child. Had the child died, then the brawlers would have lost their lives instead of their pocketbooks. I can giggle at this scenario only because no harm was done.

We can't open the index, find *miscarriage*, flip to the referenced verse, and prescribe healing for ourselves.

That pretty much covers the verses about miscarriage—except for those gems where miscarriage is a metaphor for the destruction of a rebellious nation: "Because of her guilt and her rebellion against her God, / Samaria will be punished: her people will be cut down by the sword; / Her children will be dashed to pieces; pregnant women will be torn open" (Hos. 13:16). Ouch.

At times of mourning, we need to remember (once again) that the Bible is not a medical textbook, like *Gray's Anatomy*. We can't open the index, find *miscarriage*, flip to the referenced verse, and prescribe healing for ourselves. That isn't how the Bible works because that isn't how God works. God created us to commune with Him. He wants us to know Him, and He gave us the Bible to teach us about Himself. Every story, every scripture verse, tells us something about one aspect of His character. On earth we will never be able to comprehend His righteousness because "for now, we can only see a dim and blurry picture of things, as when we stare into polished metal. . . . Everything [we] know is only part of the big picture. But one day, *when Jesus arrives,* we will see clearly, face-to-face. In that day, [we] will fully know just as [we] have been wholly known *by God*" (1 Cor. 13:12).

As we study scripture, we understand certain angles and aspects of Him and His motivations and His goals a bit better—as if we were permissibly reading the diary of a close friend. Close friends comfort us better than acquaintances because they can be sympathetic to our situations and they know what we need without us telling them. We don't expect our sisters or college roommates to have the prescription to heal our pain, so why do we treat God as if He should? His comfort comes to us when we know Him and love Him.

"There's no recipe to avoid disaster . . ."

So, what is a woman to do—tell the world you are pregnant just as soon as you know, building a potential support network if the worst happens, or wait until more people are asking why your waistline is widening than aren't and hope you never need that support network? There isn't an exact answer, but the safe road is probably straight down the middle. If you find you are pregnant, then tell those closest to you—those whom you trust. At the top of that list should be God. Let Him in on your fears, and allow Him to comfort you.

On the flip side, what if someone tells you she is six weeks pregnant? Don't fear for her; don't worry, as I tend to do. Pray for her, and pray for her baby. Remember that up to 25 percent of pregnancies end in miscarriage, and surround her with your love. Whether or not she makes the odds, you'll want to be there to mourn her tragedy or to celebrate her happy, healthy baby.

Questions

1. Are you the Facebook poster or the paranoid patient? What have you learned about timing the announcement of a pregnancy?

2. How did you process the pain of a miscarriage? Did a past miscarriage or even fear of a potential miscarriage impact your reaction to a later pregnancy?

3. Have you had a miscarriage? What were the circumstances, and how did you react physically, mentally, emotionally, and spiritually?

4. What Bible passages comfort you in times of grief?

5. What should you say and what can you do to comfort others who have lost their children due to miscarriage?

CHAPTER EIGHT

"Your Insurance Doesn't Cover That"

Paying for Your Pain, Even in Failure

As I write this chapter, our nation is experiencing the slow and cumbersome implementation of the Affordable Care Act. Open enrollment has begun for the insurance exchanges, benefits will start in 2014, and some legislators are still trying to defund the law. No matter where you fall on the political spectrum, it is obvious that this legislation will affect everyone:

- The Good: Uninsurable Americans have guaranteed access to insurance exchanges.

- The Bad: All Americans are required to spend money on medical insurance.

- The Ugly: "Just got our health and dental insurance packet for 2014 . . . where do I send my well-worded thank you letter?"[1]

What's New for 2014?

Benefit levels changing under ALL medical plans

The following medical plan changes are effective January 1.

Copay	Deductible plan	GRA plan
• Deductibles and out-of-pocket maximums are increasing • Emergency room and urgent care copays are increasing	• Out-of-network deductibles are increasing • Out-of-pocket maximums are increasing with one exception: the individual in-network OOP maximum is decreasing • Emergency room copay is increasing	• Deductibles are increasing

There are myriad reasons health insurance costs are rising across the board, not the least of which is the required implementation of the government's stated *essential health benefits*:

ambulatory patient services, emergency services, hospitalization, laboratory services, maternity and newborn care, mental health services and addiction treatment, rehabilitative services and devices, pediatric services, prescription drugs, and wellness services. If insurance companies want to be part of the government's insurance exchanges, then they are required to cover these services.[2]

Arguably the most vigorously contested piece of the Affordable Care legislation is mandatory access to birth control. Many Protestant and Catholic institutions don't want to provide birth control, and pro-life advocates fear they will be paying for others' abortions through their own premiums. The law addresses the prevention of life, but what about the creation of it? What does the ACA do for women who want to be pregnant? In a word: nothing.[3] At least nothing good. The legislation does not include infertility testing or treatment among the essential health benefits—meaning the insurance exchanges will not cover it—and the costs of private health insurance plans that may cover infertility are rising.

"We cover testing, not treatment . . ."

If you have private insurance, then you have one of four scenarios regarding infertility:

1. Nothing is covered.

2. Testing and diagnosis are covered, but no treatment is covered.

3. Testing, diagnosis, and inexpensive treatments (such as drugs) are covered.

4. Testing, diagnosis, and all treatments are covered.

Option number four is rare, not because insurance companies hate little hobbits and built their headquarters on Mount Doom, but because insurance coverage tends to lag one generation behind medical innovations.

Before the mid-1800s, the medical field was largely distrusted. Most people chose to heal at home instead of in hospitals, practices as basic as sterilization of medical instruments were not standard, and treatment costs were very low. Quite simply, health insurance was unnecessary. Health insurance as we know it today did not begin until the 1930s, approximately one generation after an explosion in medical innovation including the development of most vaccinations, the invention of X-ray machines and blood pressure cuffs, and the implementation of safety regulations. History shows that medical treatments must become routine before health insurance companies will trust the innovations enough to pay for them.

As the first IVF babies give birth to their own babies, we find ourselves at that one-generation mark, and insurance companies are slowly widening their infertility coverage. That process is a slow one because

- there is a lack of reliable statistics on the success and failure rates of treatment;

- patients might jump to costly treatments when they are unnecessary just because insurance covers them;

- multiple births are more likely in fertility patients, and those births are more costly and more dangerous;

- some high-priced treatments have low success rates.[4]

If your insurance does not pay for part or all of your infertility treatment, then get ready to lighten your wallet. Brand-new technologies are never cheap (think about the cost of your smartphone the day it first hit the stores), and that rule holds in the medical market.

"This is our price sheet for cash-only patients . . ."

Unless you have that amazing "number four" insurance, you will probably be paying for some treatment yourself. Every patient has a unique set of circumstances requiring a unique combination of drugs and procedures. It is impossible to know at the outset of your treatment exactly how much you will spend. A recent study on the cost of infertility treatments per live birth found that each successful patient would pay, on average,

- $48,424 for testing and/or surgical procedures,

- $5,894 for medications only,

- $10,696 for IUI plus Clomid,

- $19,566 for IUI plus hormone injections, and

- $61,377 for IVF.[5]

In summary, you can pay almost $50,000 finding out why you can't get pregnant and around $61,000 becoming pregnant before you even start paying all the doctors' and hospital bills every other woman incurs for prenatal care and hospital delivery.

Doctors don't run have-a-baby-or-your-money-back deals, so it is possible you will get nothing but physical and psychological pain and suffering in return for your significant financial investment. Worse than enduring month after month of negative pregnancy tests is receiving bills for surgical procedures and/or prescription drugs after a miscarriage. Medical management of an early pregnancy loss costs between $500 and $3,000,[6] and in my experience, those bills tend to arrive just as I'm feeling good enough to crawl out from under my covers for the first time.

The sticker shock is enough to keep any couple from entering fertility treatment, but can you put a price tag on family planning? Not all couples are called to adoption, and not all couples have to go all the way to IVF in order to get pregnant. Be aware of the figures, but don't let worst-case scenarios prevent you from visiting a doctor, learning what is wrong with your body, and developing a game plan. As a maid wisely advised Anne Shirley and Diana Berry in one of my favorite novels, "In this world you've just got to hope for the best and prepare for the worst and take whatever God sends."[7]

Amber's Story

When we began fertility testing four years ago, Josh and I were warned by our doctor about the emotions we were likely to face in the following months. Hormones would be running high, and she suggested that we have marital counseling in conjunction with the testing and treatment. That was a fabulous suggestion, but we didn't do it immediately because our health insurance didn't cover psychiatric appointments. I called a few offices in the Louisville area and found out it would cost us $125 out-of-pocket for each one-hour-long session. We decided to make that investment—and we are glad we did it—but the $1,500 we spent over the next year was only the first drop in a very large bucket of medical bills.

The first financial disaster hit before we had our first appointment at the fertility clinic. My regular gynecologist knew that my insurance company would pay for diagnostic testing for infertility, but that they would not cover treatment. In an attempt to save me some money and time, she ordered the basic tests, such as blood work, ultrasounds, and an HSG that any fertility center would order. She would then forward my records to the fertility clinic, assuming those tests would be cheaper when ordered by her instead of when ordered by the highly specialized fertility clinic, and hopefully saving us a clinic visit or two. I was thankful for this practical approach to the situation.

The hysterosalpingogram (a word I would be able to pronounce like a pro before my insurance battle ended) is basically a moving x-ray of the fallopian tubes. The technicians propped me up on the table, injected me with dye, and continuously x-rayed my abdomen as the dye moved through my fallopian tubes. This is a test the insurance company should cover without even blinking, regardless of who orders it. But I've come to call it my "$17,000 x-ray."

Because the gynecologist's nurses did not typically order HSGs, they had to look up its code for billing the insurance company. Someone entered the wrong code, classifying the HSG as infertility *treatment* and not gynecological testing. The first clue I had that there was a problem arrived one month after the test. My EOB came with a very long letter explaining that they would not cover fertility treatment. A week later I got my first bill from the hospital, then another from the radiologist, then a third from my gynecologist. Then they started repeating. With penalties. Every time I picked up the phone, I had to explain the scenario anew to someone I'd never spoken with before. And that person—be he or she a hospital employee or an insurance employee or one of the nurses who made the mistake in the first place—never knew what an HSG was. It took me four months of tag-you're-it phone calls to the insurance company and to the hospital, a threat from a collection agency, and finally Josh's uncomfortable conversation with his company's insurance representative to get the coding changed and the bill straightened out. We ended up paying about $2,000 for the test, hospital admittance, and reading. That was a bargain compared to what hit two weeks later.

By the time we came to a settlement over the HSG, I had been seeing a reproductive endocrinologist for three months (and paying the full $400 for each office visit, thank you very much). The doctor had reviewed all of my tests, and apart from some wacky hormone numbers, there wasn't an obvious reason for my infertility. In December 2011 I had exploratory laparoscopic surgery. The morning was a disaster from beginning to end. Hospital admittance didn't have my paperwork, I lost what must have been a pint of blood as the nurse tried to insert the IV, and my anesthesiologist was insane. I'm surprised they let him near the patients.

Don't let worst-case scenarios prevent you from visiting a doctor, learning what is wrong with your body, and developing a game plan.

Josh was sitting next to me (his chair leg in a blood smear that had escaped clean-up) when an anesthesiologist with a thick Scottish accent walked in and exclaimed to me, "Oh! You must have babies. Many, many babies!" He went on to explain that because I'm a redhead and Josh is blond, our children would be redheads. We redheads are apparently "a dying breed," and it is my duty to humanity to have as many children as possible. He then told us an off-color joke about a redheaded Catholic priest. It was a good thing the nurse had found my vein and the happy juice was flowing by then, because all I did was lie there and gape at him. Josh was just in shock. The last thing I remember is staring up into the surgical light with the anesthesiologist looking over me and explaining I'd be counting backward from one hundred. He then said something like, "So what are we having done today, Miss Amber?" looked down at the order, and went white as he realized what he'd just said to an infertility patient.

"In this world you've just got to hope for the best and prepare for the worst and take whatever God sends."

For that lovely experience, we were charged $18,000. We paid $12,000 out-of-pocket, we got an insurance "discount" of $6,000, and our insurance company paid zero. What did we get for our money? Knowledge that all my parts are in the right places (which meant the HSG was right all along), that I don't have endometriosis, and that the doctor had removed the twins I'd unknowingly carried since my body had spontaneously aborted two ectopic pregnancies. The doctors couldn't date the pregnancies because of scar tissue.

Josh and I estimate that we spent around $60,000 on fertility testing and treatment in three years. I've taken countless pills, had six rounds of IUI, five miscarriages (including my twins), two surgeries, and zero answers. When we started at the fertility clinic, the money slipped away in smallish chunks. We went into treatment thinking we could never afford adoption, so the irony that we could have adopted for the amount of money we ended up spending on failed medical treatment doesn't escape me. But Josh and I don't regret our decisions. Yes, $60,000 is a lot to spend on peace of mind, but we know we've done everything we can to get pregnant. We have never felt called to adoption—which is good since our savings account has nothing but tumbleweeds in it—but we still want children. Should God choose to bless us in the future, we'll have no doubt that it was His direct involvement that gave us a miracle.

"Get out of debt . . ."

Maybe you're like Amber, and there's "nothing but tumbleweeds" in your bank accounts. You may have also maxed out your credit cards, borrowed money from your parents, or set up a payment plan with your hospital. Whether or not your infertility treatments were successful, you have to pay those bills. It's kind of like college: you can't default on your loans just because you don't land the job you want.

It is impossible to secure your financial future if you are living underneath crushing debt, and you can't move past the pain of infertility if you're still paying doctors' bills. Remember that budget you and your spouse played with just before you married? It is time to dust it off and start living by it. Keep these very basic rules in mind:

1. Don't spend more money than you earn.

2. Keep your mortgage or rent payments under 30 percent of your income.

3. Keep all other expenses (bills, debts payments, fun money) under 50 percent of your income.

4. Save 10 percent; donate 10 percent.

If you have access to a financial advisor through your workplace, take advantage of that benefit. He or she not only can help you get out of debt as efficiently as possible, but can help you set and reach financial goals. If you can't access professional services, then just stroll through the finance section of your local bookstore. Just as there are a million diet and exercise books that cater to every personality, there's a financial strategy out there that fits your needs.

"The borrower is the slave to the lender . . ."

It is possible to learn something from any situation. David and I racked up huge bills as we tried to fix my body and have a baby. You could say that we threw that money away, but I like to think the fiscal lesson we learned was worth the money we spent. Because we budgeted to pay medical bills, we got in the habit of saving money and are now debt-free. This is not a small victory!

When David and I bought our house in 2005, we planned to live there only two years—just long enough to pay off Harvard and save for a down payment on a larger home, where we'd raise our kids. The market was hot. That wouldn't change, would it? At that two-year mark the market crashed and we owed about $20,000 more on the house than it was worth. We were stuck, and we weren't paying off Harvard quite as quickly as we thought we would. Six months later our first bill from the fertility clinic was piled on top of the mortgage and student loans.

After the market crash, David and I sat on our hands. We just couldn't decide if it was worth paying the closing costs to refinance the house. Yes, interest rates were much lower than what we were paying with our 2005 mortgage, but a refinance only paid off if we stayed here for at least three years. We weren't ready to commit to this house for that long, especially if we were going to have children.

Once we'd paid off our medical and student-loan debts, we took a hard look at our lives and admitted to ourselves that we didn't need a bigger home. We won't need a nursery. We never host out-of-town guests. In a pinch we could host a huge dinner party if we move all the furniture out of the living room. What more do we need? We refinanced, reduced our monthly payments, and knocked twelve years off the mortgage term. Totally worth paying the $1,900 in closing costs.

What does debt-freedom give you? The answer is in the question: freedom! Debts not only keep you from using your resources in the best possible ways, but they are constant reminders of the past. As long as I had a student loan, I didn't feel like a productive professional adult. As long as we had medical bills, David and I felt broken. We couldn't embark on a new life as long as we were weighed down by old debts and sad memories.

This concept of shedding the old to make way for the new is also true in the ultimate sense. Paul told the Ephesians, "You know to take off your former way of life, your *crumpled* old self—*that dark blot of a soul* corrupted by deceitful desire and lust—*to take a fresh breath* and to let God renew your

> ## It is tempting to find security in a large bank account or self-worth in an even larger mansion.

attitude and spirit" (Eph. 4:22–23). The Holy Spirit fills every Christian with new life and uses us to further God's kingdom. He doesn't want us weighed down by reminders of the past; He wants us and our resources freely at His disposal.

As you become good at budgeting and your savings account grows, it is easy to become more interested in your bank balance than in the needs of those around you. Don't go too far with your saving. The Bible talks a lot about the dangers of accumulating physical possessions and being miserly. It is tempting to find security in a large bank account or self-worth in an even larger mansion.

> **Jesus:** A wealthy man owned some land that produced a huge harvest. He often thought to himself, "I have a problem here. I don't have anywhere to store all my crops. What should I do? I know! I'll tear down

my small barns and build even bigger ones, and then I'll have plenty of storage space for my grain and all my other goods. Then I'll be able to say to myself, 'I have it made! I can relax and take it easy for years! So I'll just sit back, eat, drink, and have a good time!'" Then God interrupted the man's conversation with himself. "Excuse Me, Mr. Brilliant, but your time has come. Tonight you will die. Now who will enjoy everything you've earned and saved?" This is how it will be for people who accumulate huge assets for themselves but have no assets in relation to God. (Luke 12:16–21)

Indebtedness can keep you from blessing others—because you have no assets for Him to use—but so can hoarding. Remember that every cent you have is a gift from God, and He may have greater plans for your resources than letting them sit in a bank, gathering very little interest.

Be open to the idea that God may need to use you and your resources for His big picture (the kingdom) instead of your little picture (a family). This may mean that you never have children of your own because He needs your focus in other places. If that is the case, it is a blessing! You will find your greatest joy in being where He wants you to be and serving as He wants you to serve.

Questions

1. Have you encountered financial roadblocks to your fertility treatments? How did you address them?

2. Have you set a spending limit for your medical bills? What facts helped you determine that figure?

3. Does debt management impact your decisions?

4. Are your financial goals getting in the way of how God wants to use your resources?

CHAPTER NINE

"You Can Always Adopt"

Deciding If Adoption Is Right for You

Ever get the feeling that adoption has become trendy? Tom and Nicole did it. Angelina did it. Madonna did it. Be it domestic or international, adoption is hot in Hollywood and is becoming more common in our neighborhoods. Thanks to news media and the occasional celebrity, Westerners can know everything happening around them every moment of every day. From the AIDS epidemic in Africa to food deserts in American cities, we know we can personally effect change that saves and improves lives next door or a world away. One great way to do that is to adopt a child and give him or her a physically, emotionally, intellectually, and spiritually healthier life than that child would otherwise live. A significant investment of resources (time, love, and of course, money) in one person can impact the generations that follow that child. It is a beautiful concept and certainly one all couples should consider.

Maybe you are considering adoption. You've done the fertility thing, you've mourned the loss of children you never saw, and you now know that your child must be found and not birthed. Where do you begin?

"Your baby is out there waiting for you to find her . . ."

A debate rages. Which is better: international or domestic adoption? You will find thousands of parents on each side of the argument. Statistics for domestic adoptions are hard to develop because of the interplay between state and private adoption agencies, but according to the National Council for Adoption, there were 76,489 unrelated domestic adoptions in 2007 (the year of most recent data).[1] International adoptions have dropped from a high of 22,734 in 2005 to 8,668 in 2012.[2]

There are certainly more domestic adoptions than international, but how do you know what is best for your family? You must do a lot of research. Here are some broad statistics:

Average adoption factors	Domestic	International
Cost	$20,000–$35,000	$25,000–$50,000
Wait time	~ 1 year	≤ 4 years
Children available	> 20,000/year	≤ 10,000/year
Medical concerns	known prior to adoption	often unknown
Legal concerns	transfer of guardianship	transfer of citizenship

There are almost countless variables that impact those statistics. Before jumping to domestic adoption because you think it is cheaper or to international adoption because you think it is safer, contact a few adoption agencies. Don't rely on sensational stories you hear on the news or even the experiences of others. Do your own research. Reputable domestic agencies will tell you what to expect from the process, provide you with cost sheets, have a payment schedule based on your income level, and give you information about financial aid. Reputable international agencies will add knowledge of international law (specifically the Hague Adoption Convention) and translation services.

For more information about adoption, see the Suggested Resources section beginning on page 132.

❧ *Alexandra's Story* ❧

Sitting over dinner shortly before marrying in 1997, John and I shared our dreams of one day owning a home with a white picket fence, driving a Volvo, and having three children. We even discussed adoption. The white picket fence would have to wait, when in 1999 the U.S. military sent us on our first overseas tour to France. Our first son, Levi, was born while we lived in France; in 2000 we were blessed with a daughter, Charity. Then the miscarriages began. We had military medical, and they weren't trained in infertility support. We were deemed *subfertile*. Every doctor's attitude was, "At least you have two."

In 2003, I finally carried past the tenth week, and we were overjoyed. At twenty weeks, I kept insisting to my doctors that something wasn't right. At twenty-five weeks our son's movement slowed and then stopped. On February 5, 2004, our beautiful son Samuel was born into the world still. The only crying heard that day was ours, but the Lord heard our cries and descended His peace upon us. He blessed us with nurses who held our hands and prayed with us and a church family that reached out and loved us with words and actions.

The grief affected everyone in the family in different ways and at different times. We had a memorial service for Samuel, and it was 100 percent about glorifying God. At the service, five-year-old Levi broke down and wailed for the little brother he had prayed God would give him. What followed was the darkest year of my life. Just ten days after the delivery, my mother insisted it was time for me to get out of the house. She took me shopping, and I collapsed in the floor at Walmart and cried. I didn't care what anyone thought. Two days later a pregnant friend had a car accident and delivered her baby, and we were notified that the baby was not doing well. Another friend dragged me to the hospital to see her and talk with her. *Why am I here? Is this a cruel joke, Lord, sending me back into a maternity ward?* I soon realized why the Lord had sent me, as I knew how important it was for her to see her son and love on him. Her memories would have to last a lifetime. I was honored to meet her son and pray over him. I will cherish it for a lifetime. He went to be with the Lord the next morning. That was the first time the Lord gave me a glimpse of the impact our son's short life and our testimony would and could have.

I spent the next one and a half years seeing everything. God sent women to me—He still does—and I physically felt for the women, each with her own story of loss. I started a ministry at our church making burial gowns for babies, I led a support group at the hospital, and I healed through sharing Samuel's story. I learned that we must grieve. I learned not to ask Him, *Why?* but to ask Him, *For what purpose?* Walk through your grief; God wants to get you on the other side. He wants to commune with you during these times. If you don't walk with Him, you'll be knocking at the doorway to peace forever.

After another miscarriage because of low HCG, John and I knew we would divorce if we didn't stop the roller coaster ride of trying to get pregnant. We decided we were done trying to have kids and went on vacation. We thanked God for each of the children he had blessed us with.

Six weeks later I was pregnant with Thomas. Because we never found a problem with Samuel before he passed, I worried constantly about Thomas and was poked and prodded by the doctors.

At week twenty-eight, after another sleepless night, I gave my unborn son back to the Lord and said to Him, "He is yours, Lord, and I give him to Your keeping." That was my moment of total surrender. I was in tears on my knees that night. At thirty-five weeks pregnant they found I had a cord prolapse and Thomas was breach. John called the church and started an immediate prayer chain. An

I learned not to ask Him, Why? but to ask Him, For what purpose?

emergency C-section was performed. The same angel nurses who had been with me for Samuel's delivery stood beside me during the surgery. There was not a dry eye in the room when he took his first breath. As Thomas was wheeled to the NICU, my son asked Grandma if "God would let us keep this baby." She answered truthfully that she didn't know. After eight days, we brought our son home and rejoiced.

When Thomas was five months old, we moved to Panama. There were two adoptive families assigned on the base with us, and we felt a long-quenched calling to adopt rising again. We were about to learn that adoption is its own kind of pregnancy; there are ups and downs, stacks of money, months of paperwork. It would take us three years to bring our first adopted daughter home, and tons of faith.

As we walked the long journey of the paperwork and the daunting task of saving for funds for our daughter's adoption, God kept asking us to trust Him. "Just TRUST me," He whispered. God moved mountains all along the way, and right at the end of the adoption process, we figured out unexpectedly that we were four thousand dollars short. We had applied for a grant from Show

Hope, Steven Curtis Chapman's adoption aid charity, but the mail between Panama and the United States tends to be delayed. When John e-mailed to find out the status of the grant, we learned it had been granted eight weeks earlier, in the exact amount of four thousand dollars. We traveled to China to meet Joy, and on October 10, 2008, she was placed in our arms for the first time—a fragile, sick, frightened eighteen-month-old who needed us as much as we needed her. The Lord continued to minister to our every need as we walked the journey of healing our daughter's neglected soul.

Since then God has sent us two more beautiful Chinese waiting children: Caleb and Faith. Caleb's adoption was about obedience. We felt God telling us that he was ours, but the timing was inconvenient and the calling seemed irrational. *We already have five children,* we said to ourselves. *Raising children is expensive, Lord,* we reasoned. But we did as God told us, and Caleb's transition was beautiful. He'd had excellent foster parents in China, and I thank God for them to this day. He is a happy, easygoing little boy who is eager to learn and praise God.

Faith's adoption was about just that: faith. I learned online that there had been a "disruption" in her adoption by a family living in

This mixture of "biological" and adopted children was now supposed to demonstrate God's greatness to the rest of the world.

Nevada. They had successfully brought her to the United States from China, but Faith was not blending with their family. God has given me discernment for children's true condition, and I just knew that she was meant to be ours. It took three years to bring our Joy home; it took about three weeks to bring our Faith home, thanks to prayers and a wonderful social worker. We tell Faith that God used that family to bring her to us, and I fully believe that. She brightens each and every day and is truly a ray of sunshine in our lives.

Little did we know that those dreams we had so many years ago were just the beginning of the journey God had for us. We never planned to be parents to six children here on earth, and we still don't have a white picket fence or a Volvo. What we do have is a family comprising six blessings, each with his or her own birth story, who have all been Chosen, Adopted, and Redeemed by our Savior, Jesus Christ.

"God adopted you and me."

When God created our universe, it was perfect. God walked on earth with us. No one needed to be saved from anything because fruit from the Tree of Life made us immortal. Then Adam and Eve messed things up for the rest of us by breaking the one rule God had given them: don't eat from the Tree of Knowledge of Good and Evil. From that moment forward, we all needed to be saved from the evil separating us from the good God.

Much later God set apart one family—Abraham's descendants through Isaac and then Jacob—as His special children. The Israelites, as they would be known, were supposed to demonstrate God's greatness so that through their example, the rest of the world would be saved too. God gave them a set of laws that guided their knowledge of good and evil and, if followed perfectly, would save them from the effects of sin. God started with ten, but by the time He had detailed the laws to His children's satisfaction, there were 613. That's a lot of laws, and generation after generation, God's children failed to follow those laws and avoid evil as perfectly as they should. The kids would misbehave, God would discipline them, they'd straighten up, and the cycle would begin again.

By the time Jesus came, God's children were known as the Jews, and they weren't representing their Father any better than their ancestors had. They needed saving just as badly as everyone else did. Once Jesus came, anyone who believed His sacrifice was enough to cover all the evil Adam and Eve had let into the world was adopted into God's family—regardless of who their ancestors were. Abraham's kids were no longer God's only children: family membership was now open to the rest of the world.

Shortly after Jesus' sacrifice, Paul wrote about this concept of adoption into God's family to the Romans, Galatians, and Ephesians. His audiences were churches in non-Jewish areas of the Roman Empire who were trying to understand how God's people—Jewish and adopted—are set apart from the rest of the world. This mixture of "biological" and adopted children was now supposed to demonstrate God's greatness to the rest of the world. His messages to the three cities were similar:

1. God sent His Son to the world as a sacrifice.

2. That sacrifice sealed a new covenant between God and humanity.

3. The covenant states that those indwelt by the Holy Spirit are freed from slavery to the law and are children of God.

4. God's children will inherit His kingdom alongside Jesus.

Paul wrote:

If the Spirit of God is leading you, then *take comfort in knowing* you are His children. You see, you have not received a spirit that returns you to slavery, so you have nothing to fear. The Spirit you have received adopts you *and welcomes you* into God's own family. That's why we call out to Him, "Abba! Father!" *as we would address a loving daddy. Through that prayer,* God's Spirit confirms in our spirits that we are His children. If we are God's children, that means we are His heirs along with the Anointed, set to inherit everything that is His. If we share His sufferings, *we know that* we will ultimately share in His glory. (Rom. 8:14–17)

When the right time arrived, God sent His Son into this world (born of a woman, subject to the law) to free those who, *just like Him,* were subject to the law. Ultimately He wanted us all to be adopted as sons and daughters. Because you are now part of God's family, He sent the Spirit of His Son into our hearts; *and the Spirit* calls out, "Abba, Father." You no longer have to live as a slave because you are a child *of God.* And since you are His child, God guarantees an inheritance *is waiting* for you. (Gal. 4:4–7)

God chose us to be in a relationship with Him even before He laid out plans for this world; He wanted us to live holy lives characterized by love, *free from sin,* and blameless before Him. He destined us to be adopted as His children through *the covenant* Jesus the Anointed *inaugurated in His sacrificial life.* This was His pleasure and His will *for us.* (Eph. 1:4–5)

The idea that anyone—regardless of parentage or class or race—could be a member of God's family and enjoy the benefits His "biological" children had was plausible to (though probably unexpected by) the new Christians. Adoption was a common practice among the upper classes in the Roman world. If a senatorial family had no sons, they would find a family with too many sons and adopt one of them as heir. In fact, the very people reading these letters may have been alive during the highest-profile adoption ever to occur in Rome: Julius Caesar adopted his grandnephew, Octavian, as his son and heir. Octavian was of course Augustus Caesar, the Roman emperor when Jesus was crucified.

God could have saved humanity by any method, but He chose to model adoption. His adopted children (non-Jews) are no more or less loved than His "biological" children (the Israelites and Jews). They have no greater or lesser inheritance. Anyone who receives the Holy Spirit is God's child and will inherit the kingdom.

"Adoption is always the right thing to do . . ."

Adoption is obviously a God-approved method of family building, but you shouldn't adopt only because you can't have biological offspring. An adopted child is not a consolation prize.

Because adoption is a frequent topic in our culture, it's not uncommon for people to expect a couple struggling to conceive a child will choose to build their family through adoption. Obtaining a child has, to some degree, become a goal for the couple, and adoption is a way to achieve

> ### God could have saved humanity by any method, but He chose to model adoption.

that goal. This idea that adoption is "plan *b*" comes from the unconscious confluence of two ideas: somehow having a baby is the only way you'll be happy, and not adopting when you have no biological children is selfish. Neither idea is necessarily correct, and both can leave you feeling sad and guilty.

I would argue that adoption is a calling, and it is possible that God is not calling you to adopt. At the moment He is not calling David and me to adopt. When you become a parent of a biological or adopted child, your priorities must change. You have less time to serve God in ways other than child-rearing because you are raising and teaching and loving your child(ren). This is a high calling, but it is not God's plan for everyone.

Consider for a moment that your desire to raise children may have a nontraditional application. God may be calling you to mentor in other ways—such as teaching a Sunday school class or being a Big Sister—that will actually impact a quantity of people. Maybe God wants to use your money to help send your nieces and nephews or godsons and goddaughters to college. Maybe He wants to move you to a new place where you wouldn't want to take your children. Maybe He wants you to stay in the workforce. Or maybe He wants you to adopt! The point is, God has a plan for your life that fits perfectly with His will. Before you jump to adoption—or feel guilty for not adopting—pray. Ask God how He wants to use you to impact the next generation. It may be in ways you never would have imagined.

Questions

1. Do you feel pressured to adopt? How can you respond?

2. Are you more drawn to international or domestic adoption? Why?

3. Knowing that God models adoption, are you more likely to consider it?

4. Is God calling you to adopt, or do you see adoption as a consolation prize?

CHAPTER TEN

"You Never Know What God Will Do"

Moving Forward

I love history. I am academically trained as a biblical archaeologist, I read biographies and history books for fun, and I am fully aware that the "good ole days" are always in the past—whether you're looking back from 2014 or from 1814. (Notice I waited until the end of the book to confess what a geek I truly am!) I come by this love of all things past naturally. My father wanted to be a history professor, and his mother loved to regale our family (and anyone else trapped in the room) with often-inaccurate stories of our supposed ancestors. In 1998 Granny Womack was caught on tape bragging to an in-law that our family is "directly descended from Dolley Madison." Why she chose to name-drop Dolley instead of James, none of us have ever figured out. Maybe she was craving baked goods at the time.

Granny Womack learned most of her stories from our family's matriarch, Elizabeth Hope Snell Jackson Deans, known to our family as "Bess" or "Aunt Bessie." Just before her first marriage to Glenn Jackson (a direct descendant of Andrew Jackson, Granny would have told you), my great-grandaunt had inherited a Victorian steamer trunk and subsequently filled it with family memorabilia that verifies and expands on some of the stories Granny would so frequently tell us grandkids about the Snell family of the 1900s and about her own childhood years when Aunt Bessie raised her. Aunt Bessie died when I was three years old, and I am sorry that my only memory is of her lying very sick in her bed. Not knowing her makes me all the more grateful for Granny's and Daddy's stories—which have taught me that she was the most amazing woman ever to host a dinner party in Charlotte County, Virginia. (That indisputable fact certainly is not informed by the coincidence that I am her namesake.) She was the daughter of a Civil War-era doctor who grew into a statuesque woman—five feet, nine inches tall and beautiful—and who graduated from college with an advanced medical degree in a time when women did not pursue higher education.

As I was struggling to have children in the late 2000s, my Granny Womack was losing her battle with Alzheimer's, diabetes, and COPD. The day after she died, we grandkids went through her and Papa's house, looking for old pictures to make a photo montage of her life for the visitation and funeral. It is easy to lose direction when working on a project such as that one; I was quickly sidetracked by all the early-twentieth-century letters I found in (what has become) our family's Victorian steamer trunk. The letters, which I inherited just before my Papa's death in February 2014, have now introduced me to the strong feminine soul behind the family stories and have taught me just how much I have in common with the other *Hope*ful woman in my family.

Elizabeth Hope's Story

In 1936 Bess and Glenn Jackson were living in the overseer's house on the remnants of her family's plantation, Locust Grove, when she received a letter from her brother, Peyton. He and his wife, Mary, had two daughters, a toddler named Ann Madison and an infant named Betty Lee. The Great Depression and his subsequent alcoholism had taken most of Peyton's resources, and he was unable to support both of his daughters. He asked Bess to raise Ann Madison because the Jacksons were a rare two-income household: Glenn was a radio sportscaster; Bess was a nurse. Bess and Glenn had been married several years, but they were frequently separated as he traveled the country with sports teams and she traveled the state of Virginia as a nurse. They certainly weren't ready to parent a toddler. But Bess and Glenn fell in love with Ann Madison, and during those six years when they raised her niece, Bess was unable to have a child of her own.

Tragedy struck the family on April 9, 1942, when Glenn died suddenly at a radio station in Greensboro, North Carolina. Bess asked her older half sister Clara (who had been a mother figure to Bess, Peyton, and their sister Ann when their own mother had died) to come live at Locust Grove with her and Ann Madison. Clara would maintain the farm and raise Ann Madison while Bess traveled Virginia with her job. The three ladies, young and old, had a blissful summer; Ann Madison could "do no wrong" in Clara's eyes. But in November 1942, Peyton requested that Ann Madison be returned to him. A brilliant chemist when he could stay away from liquor, he had secured a new job and a new home and had sent six-year-old Betty Lee to boarding school; he and Mary had time and money for their eldest daughter again. He wrote, "We [Peyton and Mary] are neither of us forgetting yours and Glenn's kindness and help to us, but Bess[,] we just couldn't give up A. M. for good. I am more than sorry to have upset you and Clara both."[1]

Peyton and Bess's sister Ann was working as a nurse in Philadelphia when she heard the news of Peyton's request. She sent a lengthy letter to Peyton and Mary, thinly veiling a threat to help Bess and Clara sue them for full custody of Ann Madison. On the typed copy of the letter she mailed to her sisters, Ann handwrote, "Bess, I took the liberty of writing this. Hope you and C.

won't mind too much. I am advising her not to sue [for custody], but let them get A. M. Consult a lawyer if you wish. With his record [of

In my aunt's life I see an example of the path I should travel as a "barren" woman.

public drunkenness] and the paper [he sent to Bess and Glenn requesting their help raising Ann Madison], you may have a case. Will write tomorrow. A."[2]

Before Christmas, Peyton came and claimed his eight-year-old daughter, ripping her from the only home and the only mother she'd ever known.

For the next ten years, Bess looked forward to when Ann Madison—and occasionally Betty Lee—would return to the farm to spend her summer vacation with the sisters. This ended the year Ann Madison turned eighteen, married, and started a family of her own.

Bess was a state health nurse who specialized in tuberculosis control. Herself a tuberculosis survivor, she dedicated her life to the prevention and treatment of the disease. She traveled to a different Virginia county Monday through Wednesday, and she worked in Richmond Thursday and Friday of every week.

One night in 1953, Bess was attacked and raped as she was going into her home at Locust Grove. The independent spirit that had enabled her to work as a medical professional and survive the tragic loss of her husband was shaken by this incident. Initially unable to cope with her newfound fear of the world, Bess married Kelly, a retired merchant marine who could give her the safety she needed, if not the love she missed. As she always did, Bess overcame the tragedy, though it hardened her just a bit.

A few years later Bess found herself raising a new generation of nieces and nephews. Ann Madison's son Ross became a permanent fixture in Bess and Kelly's home every summer. On the days he wasn't sailing with Kelly in Norfolk, Ross was running around the city of Richmond, waiting for Aunt Bessie to finish her shift at the hospital. She did her best to teach him manners, but Ross was better off on the sea than in a Charlotte County dining room. In spite of reminding him to be on his best behavior, Ross once vomited clabbered milk—an old Virginian delicacy—across a socialite's lunch table. Aunt Bessie was thoroughly embarrassed, and her reputation as the best cook in the county was replaced by this anecdote about her unruly grandnephew.

As did his mother before him, Ross loved Aunt Bessie as much more than an aunt. She was a grandmother to him, closer to him than Ann Madison's own mother was. When she died in 1984, Bessie left a legacy of love, strength, and decorum. Through her medical work, she had treated countless tuberculosis patients. Because of her love, she had raised Ann Madison and become the matriarch of a family that was not her own but that wouldn't have thrived without her.

Do you see why I enjoy biographies? They tend to be great stories that are entertaining and instructive. In my aunt's life I see an example of the path I should travel as a "barren" woman: God called Aunt Bessie to sacrifice herself for tuberculosis patients and for her family. She served Him well. As a result of her service to her family, He surrounded her with more family. Those children may not have been her flesh-and-blood babies, but they considered her to be a mother, and their children still refer to her as the family matriarch. What a legacy.

"Don't be afraid . . ."

I admit it: part of why I wanted children was that I feared not having them. I wondered, *Who will care for me in my old age?* I'm an only child. I don't want to end up alone and forgotten. This, of course, is not a good reason to have a baby. Fear should never motivate any decision.

In his last letter to Timothy, Paul told his young disciple—and us—that fear and cowardice do not come from God: "What strikes me most is how *natural and* sincere your faith is. I am convinced that the same faith that dwelt in your grandmother, Lois, and your mother, Eunice, abides in you as well. This is why I *write to* remind you to stir up the gift of God that *was conveyed* to you when I laid my hands upon you. You see, God did not give us a cowardly spirit but a powerful, loving, and disciplined spirit" (2 Tim. 1:5–7).

I long to be told that my faith is "sincere," that it is the same faith that lived in my great grandaunt Bessie. Her spirit was indeed "powerful, loving, and disciplined." When her first husband died, when she was raped, when she knew for certain she'd never have a child of her own, Aunt Bessie thrived because she knew what I'm slowing learning: God will always be with me; I can't ever be alone.

In the immediate future (and I hope for decades to come), I have my husband, David, to literally keep me company. I am so thankful for him, but just as a child could never satisfy my life, David cannot either. David is not the source of my strength, the silencer of my fears. God is. Only God will always be with me. Because I am His adopted daughter, God's Spirit lives inside me.

Paul may have gone so far as to say that my David is an impediment to my relationship with God. When he wrote to the church at Corinth, he addressed interpersonal relationships and corrected some wrong behaviors. He sent his advice to edify the church and the individuals within it.

My primary desire is for you to be free from the worries *that plague humanity*. A single man can focus on the things of the Lord and how to please the Lord, but a married man has to worry about the details of the here and now and how to please his wife. A married man will always have divided loyalties. *The same idea is true for* a young unmarried woman. She concerns herself only with the work of the Lord and how to dedicate herself entirely, body and spirit, *to her Lord*. On the other hand, a married woman has vast responsibilities for her family and a desire to please her husband. I am not trying to give you more rules and regulations. I only want to give you advice that is fitting and helpful. I want to help you live lives of faithful devotion to the Lord without any distraction (1 Cor. 7:32–35).

Paul says it is preferable not to marry because family relationships divide our "loyalties" and keep us from wholly dedicating our lives to God. This is not a contradiction to "Be fruitful and multiply. Populate the

> ## Having a baby isn't a happy ending; at most it's a stop along the path. Finding wholeness by accepting God's plan is a happy ending!

earth" (Gen. 1:28), the very verse with which I began this book and the verse that has given millennia of infertile women their inferiority complexes.

Paul models a celibate life spent in service to God, but we don't have to be celibate to serve God. A celibate life results in a life without children, but parents serve God every day inside and outside their homes. Paul was speaking from his own experiences, suggesting that the fewer ties we have on earth, the closer we can follow God and the more we can do for His kingdom. He calls some of His children to be parents, but not others. We are all necessary in the church.

"You are fruitful."

I suppose the clichéd happy ending to this book would be me sharing with the world that I, too, am having a baby. But that won't be happening, and that is really the antithesis of the message. Having a baby isn't a happy ending; at most it's a stop along the path. Finding wholeness by accepting God's plan is a happy ending!

The next time you feel the full weight of the word *barren*, remember that children aren't the only "fruit" in the Bible. Ironically I learned this truth as a child by memorizing a child's song. I can still see my VBS teacher, Miss Susan, animatedly leading the room in a chorus of

> The fruit of the Spirit's not a [insert your favorite fruit here]!
> If you wanna be a [insert your favorite fruit here],
> you might as well hear it:
> you can't be a fruit of the Spirit
> 'Cause the fruits are
> love, joy, peace, patience,
> kindness, goodness, faithfulness,
> gentleness, and self-con-trol-ol-ol![3]

My favorite fruit to sing about was always the lemon. We got to pucker our lips and squint our eyes as if we'd just tasted something sour.

Paul was more earnest as he described to the people of Galatia the Holy Spirit's fruits and the culture they can create among people whose lives are dedicated to God's work:

The Holy Spirit produces a different kind of fruit: *unconditional* love, joy, peace, patience, kindheartedness, goodness, faithfulness, gentleness, and self-control. You won't find any law opposed to fruit like this. Those of us who belong to the Anointed One have crucified our old lives and put to death the flesh and all the lusts and desires that plague us.

Now since we have chosen to walk with the Spirit, let's keep each step in perfect sync with God's Spirit. This will happen when we set aside our self-interests *and work together to create true community* instead of a culture consumed by provocation, *pride,* and envy. (Gal. 5:22–26)

The Holy Spirit's fruit is independent of physiology. It is produced in our lives when we walk in lockstep with Him, making His one will (humanity's reconciliation with Him) our one will. Accept that His plan for our lives has one purpose: to help others find reconciliation. It is a self-less mission He gives to His children, but it is not without rewards. How many of us spend time praying for the fruit—love, joy, peace, patience, kindness, goodness, faithfulness, gentleness, and self-control—when we should be praying for more of His Spirit? Walk closely with God, and turn your circumstances on their head. Be spiritually fruitful in a barren world.

Questions

1. Are you *afraid* you'll never have children?

2. Do any of your relationships keep you from walking in lockstep with God?

3. What is the fruit in your life?

4. What will it take for you to be fruitful in a barren world?

Suggested Resources

For Marriage Support

LaHaye, Tim and Beverly. *The Act of Marriage: The Beauty of Sexual Love*, rev. ed. Grand Rapids: Zondervan, 1998.

Tournier, Paul. *To Understand Each Other*. Translated by John S. Gilmour. Atlanta: John Knox, 1967.

For Lifestyle Modifications

GoodGuide. http://www.goodguide.com

Krissoff, Liana. *Canning for a New Generation: Bold, Fresh Flavors for the Modern Pantry*. New York: Abrams, 2010.

LocalHarvest: Real Food, Real Farmers, Real Community. http://www. localharvest.org/csa

Reno, Tosca. *The Eat-Clean Diet Recharged*. Mississauga, ON: Robert Kennedy, 2009.

For Emotional Education

Clark, Lynn. *SOS: Help for Emotions: Managing Anxiety, Anger, and Depression*. Bowling Green, KY: SOS Programs and Parents Press, 1998.

Cloud, Henry, and John Townsend. *Boundaries: When to Say Yes, How to Say No to Take Control of Your Life*. Grand Rapids: Zondervan, 1992.

For Adoption Research

Administration for Children and Families. https://www.acf.hhs.gov

Grant, Jennifer. *Love You More: The Divine Surprise of Adopting My Daughter*. Nashville: Thomas Nelson, 2011.

Notes

Chapter 1

1. Rakesh Sharma et al., "Lifestyle factors and reproductive health: taking control of your fertility," *Reproductive Biology and Endocrinology* 11, no. 66 (2013): 2, http://www.rbej.com/content/11/1/66.

2. Pedro Acién and Irene Velasco, "Endometriosis: A Disease That Remains Enigmatic," *ISRN Obstetrics and Gynecology* 2013 (2013): 1, http://www.hindawi.com/journals/isrn.obgyn/2013/242149/.

3. Bulent Demir et al., "An Incidental Finding of Unicornuate Uterus with Unilateral Ovarian Agenesis During Cesarean Delivery," *Archives of Gynecology and Obstetrics* 276, no. 1 (2007): 91–93, doi: 10.1007/s00404-006-0317-x

4. Nina Madnani et al., "Polycystic ovarian syndrome," *Indian Journal of Dermatology, Venereology, and Leprology* 79, no. 3 (2013): 310–21.

5. Hayley S. Quant et al., "Reproductive implications of psychological distress for couples undergoing IVF," *Journal of Assisted Reproduction and Genetics* 30, no. 8 (September 2013): 1451–58; Germaine M. Buck et al., "Stress Reduces Conception Probabilities across the Fertile Window: Evidence in Support of Relaxation," *Fertility and Sterility* 95, no. 7 (June 2011): 2184–89.

Chapter 2

1. Marie E. Thoma et al., "Prevalence of infertility in the United States as estimated by the current duration approach and a traditional constructed approach," *Fertility and Sterility* 99, no. 5 (April 2013): 1327.

2. Elizabeth Comeau, "A First for the First," *Boston Globe*, August 6, 2001.

3. European Society of Human Reproduction and Embryology, "The world's number of IVF and ICSI babies has now reached a calculated total of 5 million," news release, July 2, 2012, http://www.eshre.eu/press-room/press-releases/press-releases-eshre-2012/5-million-babies.aspx.

4. Aleida G. Huppelschoten et al., "Improving patient-centeredness of fertility care using a multifaceted approach: study protocol for a randomized controlled trial," *Trials* 13 (2012): 175, http://www.trialsjournal.com/content/13/1/175.

5. L. Lechner, C. Bolman, and A. van Dalen, "Definite involuntary childlessness: associations between coping, social support and psychological distress," *Human Reproduction* 22, no. 1 (2007): 288–94, available online at http://www. researchgate.net/ publication/6866949_Definite_involuntary_childlessness_associations_ between_coping_social_support_and_psychological_distress.

6. Henry Cloud and John Townsend, *Boundaries: When to Say Yes, How to Say No to Take Control of Your Life* (Grand Rapids: Zondervan, 1992).

Chapter 3

1. W. D. Mosher and W. F. Pratt, "Fecundity and infertility in the United States: Incidence and trends," *Fertility and Sterility* 56 (1991):192–93.

2. L. W. Roth, A. R. Ryan, and R. B. Meacham, "Clomiphene citrate in the management of male infertility," *Seminars in Reproductive Medicine* 31, no. 4 (July 2013): 245–50, http://www.ncbi.nlm.nih.gov/pubmed/23775379.

3. James F. Smith et al., "Sexual, Marital, and Social Impact of a Man's Perceived Infertility Diagnosis," *Journal of Sexual Medicine* 6, no. 9 (September 2009): 2505–15; available online at http://onlinelibrary.wiley.com/ doi/10.1111/j.1743-6109.2009.01383.x/abstract.

4. John Schwartz, "Billy Crystal Reads for an Audience, Prompting Laughter and a Surprise," *ArtsBeat* (blog), June 28, 2013, http://artsbeat.blogs.nytimes. com/2013/06/28/ billy-crystal-reads-for-an-audience-prompting-laughter-and-a-surprise/.

5. *Forget Paris*, directed by Billy Crystal (1995; Atlanta: Turner Home Entertainment, 2000), DVD.

6. A. Martin Matthews and R. Matthews, "Beyond the Mechanics of Infertility: Perspectives on the Social Psychology of Infertility and Involuntary Childlessness," *Family Relations* 35, no. 4 (1986): 579–87.

7. A. J. Farley, "What Do We Do with the Doubts of Job?" (sermon, New Heights Chapel, Murfreesboro, TN, February 26, 2012).

Chapter 4

1. N. A. Clark et al., "A systematic review of the evidence for complementary and alternative medicine in infertility," *International Journal of Gynecology and Obstetrics* 122, no. 3 (September 2013):202–6; available online at http://www. ncbi.nlm.nih.gov/pubmed/23796256.

Chapter 5

1. Melanie Hicken, "Average Cost to Raise a Kid: $241,080," CNNMoney, August 14, 2013, http://money.cnn.com/2013/08/14/pf/cost-children/.

2. Sam De Coster and Nicolas van Larebeke, "Endocrine-Disrupting Chemicals: Associated Disorders and Mechanisms of Action," *Journal of Environmental and Public Health* 2012: 38, http://www.hindawi.com/journals/jeph/2012/713696/.

3. Kiyah J. Duffey and Barry M. Popkin, "High-fructose corn syrup: is this what's for dinner?" *American Journal of Clinical Nutrition* 88, no. 6 (December 2008): 1722S–32S; available online at http://ajcn.nutrition.org/content/88/6/1722S.short.

4. Eric Kripke, Andrew Dabb, and Daniel Loflin, "There Will Be Blood," *Supernatural*, season 7, episode 22, directed by Guy Norman Bee, aired May 11, 2012 (Burbank: Warner, 2012), DVD.

5. Walter J. Crinnion, "Toxic Effects of the Easily Avoidable Phthalates and Parabens," *Alternative Medicine Review* 15, no. 3 (2010):190–96.

6. "Shout Triple Acting Trigger," GoodGuide, http://www.goodguide.com/products/293505-shout-triple-acting-trigger; accessed May 9, 2014.

7. *The Novels of Jane Austen: Persuasion*, vol. 10 (Edinburgh: John Grant, 1905), 120.

8. Rakesh Sharma et al., "Lifestyle factors and reproductive health: taking control of your fertility," *Reproductive Biology and Endocrinology* 11, no. 66 (2013); http://www.rbej.com/content/11/1/66.

Chapter 6

1. Jenna Goudreau, "Women Beat Men in Advanced Degrees," *Forbes*, April 27, 2011, http://www.forbes.com/sites/jennagoudreau/2011/04/27/women-beat-men-in-advanced-degrees/.

2. *Highlights of Women's Earnings in 2011*, report 1038 (Washington: Bureau of Labor Statistics, 2012), http://www.bls.gov/cps/cpswom2011.pdf, 1, 2.

3. Lauren Weber, "Why Dads Don't Take Paternity Leave," *Wall Street Journal*, June 12, 2013, http://online.wsj.com/news/articles/SB10001424127887324049504578541633708283670.

4. Henry Cloud, *How to Get a Date Worth Keeping: Be Dating in Six Months or Your Money Back* (Grand Rapids: Zondervan, 2005), 27.

5. B. E. Hamilton et al., "Annual summary of vital statistics: 2010–2011," *Pediatrics* 131 (2013): 548–58; available online at http://pediatrics. aappublications.org/content/early/2013/02/05/peds.2012-3769.abstract.

6. Rakesh Sharma et al., "Lifestyle factors and reproductive health: taking control of your fertility," *Reproductive Biology and Endocrinology* 11, no. 66 (2013): 2, http://www.rbej.com/content/11/1/66.

7. "The Costs of Infertility Treatment," *Resolve: The National Infertility Association*, http://www.resolve.org/family-building-options/insurance_coverage/the-costs-of-infertility-treatment.html; accessed May 9, 2014.

8. Laura Bell, "What happens to extra embryos after IVF?" *CNN Health*, September 1, 2009, http://www.cnn.com/2009/HEALTH/09/01/extra.ivf. embryos/index.html?iref=24hours.

Chapter 7

1. "Miscarriage," *American Pregnancy Association*, http://americanpregnancy.org/ pregnancycomplications/miscarriage.html; updated. November 2011.

2. Sharon P. Rodrigues et al., "Ectopic pregnancy: when is expectant management safe?" *Journal of Gynecological Surgery* 9, no. 4 (November 2012): 421–26 http://www.ncbi.nlm.nih.gov/pmc/articles/PMC3491186/.

3. *The Help*, directed by Tate Taylor (2011; Burbank: Buena Vista, 2011), DVD.

4. Kathryn Stockett, *The Help* (New York: Putnam, 2009), 237

5. Ibid., 405.

Chapter 8

1. Melissa Teply's Facebook page, accessed October 18, 2013, https://www. facebook.com/melissa.teply.9?fref=ts.

2. "10 Health Care Benefits Covered in the Health Insurance Marketplace," *HealthCare.gov* (blog), August 22, 2013, https://www.healthcare.gov/ blog/10-health-care-benefits-covered-in-the-health-insurance-marketplace/.

3. Nitya Rajeshuni, "Infertility: A Plague Gone Unnoticed," *Stanford Journal of Public Health* 3, no. 1 (Winter 2013), 27–32, http://www.scribd.com/ doc/132143247/ Stanford-Journal-of-Public-Health-Volume-3-Issue-1-Winter-2013.

4. "A History of IVF," International Council on Infertility Information Dissemination, http://www.inciid.org/printpage.php?cat=ivf&id=465; accessed May 10, 2014.

·

5. Patricia Katz et al., "Costs of infertility treatment: Results from an 18-month prospective cohort study," *Fertility and Sterility* 95, no. 3 (March 1, 2011): 921; available online at http://www.fertstert.org/article/S0015-0282(10)02812-8/abstract.

6. Mary Rausch et al., "A Cost-Effectiveness Analysis of Surgical Versus Medical Management of Early Pregnancy Loss," *Fertility and Sterility* 97, no. 2 (February 2012): 355–60.e1, http://fertstertforum.com/201297355rausch/.

7. Lucy Maud Montgomery, *Anne of Avonlea* (1909; London: Sovereign, 2012), 222.

Chapter 9

1. Paul J. Placek, "National Adoption Data Assembled by the National Council for Adoption," http://archive.poughkeepsiejournal.com/assets/pdf/BK205214511.pdf.

2. "Statistics," Intercountry Adoption, Bureau of Consular Affairs, U. S. Department of State, http://adoption.state.gov/about_us/statistics.php; accessed May 10, 2014.

Chapter 10

1. James Peyton Snell to Mrs. Glenn E. Jackson, Rich Creek, VA, November 13, 1942, private collection.

2. Annie M. Snell to Mrs. Glenn E. Jackson, Philadelphia, November 4, 1942, private collection.

3. Fruit of the Spirit song. Writer Unknown.

❧ About the Author ❧

Amanda Hope Haley enjoys hosting people in her home for small group studies and serving her church community however she can. Amanda loves cooking, crafting, and party planning, but she's happiest when exploring new places with her husband, David, and spoiling her godsons, Elijah and Jack.

Amanda has a bachelor of arts in religious studies from Rhodes College and a master of theological studies in Hebrew Scripture and Interpretation from Harvard University. She contributed to The Voice Bible translation as a writer and editor, and she has been an editor and curricula ghostwriter for popular Christian authors. Today she contributes to *Living in Exile*, a weekly podcast for people who are "in the world but not of the world," and "in the Church but not of the church." Amanda also maintains a blog, *Healthy and Hopeful*, where she encourages women to live whole lives in community with God, family, and each other. Amanda and David recently moved to Denver, Colorado, and look forward to new friends and new adventures out West.

SHARE THE INSCRIBED COLLECTION

EXPERIENCE THE BOOKS

Your friends can sample this book or any of our InScribed titles for FREE. Visit InScribedStudies.com and select any of our titles to learn how.

Know a church, ministry, or small group that would benefit from these readings? Contact your favorite bookseller or visit InScribedStudies.com/buy-in-bulk for bulk purchasing information.

CONNECT WITH THE AUTHORS

Do you want to get to know more about the author of this book or any of the authors in the InScribed Collection? Go online to InScribedStudies.com to see how you could meet them through a Google Hangout or connect with them through our InScribed Facebook.

JOIN IN THE CONVERSATION

 Like facebook.com/InScribedStudies and be the first to see new videos, discounts, and updates from the InScribed Studies team.

 Start following @InScribedStudy.

 Follow our author's boards @InScribedStudies.

WWW.INSCRIBEDSTUDIES.COM